D1360417

PHP and MySQL™

P H R A S E B O O K

Christian Wenz

✦Addison-Wesley

Developer's Library

Upper Saddle River, NJ · Boston · Indianapolis · San Francisco
New York · Toronto · Montreal · London · Munich · Paris · Madrid
Cape Town · Sydney · Tokyo · Singapore · Mexico City

PHP and MySQL™ Phrasebook

Copyright © 2013 by Pearson Education, Inc.

ISBN-13: 978-0-321-83463-8

ISBN-10: 0-321-83463-1

The Library of Congress Cataloging-in-Publication Data is on file.

Printed in the United States of America

First Printing: October 2012

Trademarks

All terms mentioned in this book that are known to be trademarks or service marks have been appropriately capitalized. Pearson cannot attest to the accuracy of this information. Use of a term in this book should not be regarded as affecting the validity of any trademark or service mark.

Warning and Disclaimer

Every effort has been made to make this book as complete and as accurate as possible, but no warranty or fitness is implied. The information provided is on an "as is" basis. The author and the publisher shall have neither liability nor responsibility to any person or entity with respect to any loss or damages arising from the information contained in this book.

Bulk Sales

Pearson offers excellent discounts on this book when ordered in quantity for bulk purchases or special sales. For more information, please contact

U.S. Corporate and Government Sales

1-800-382-3419

corpsales@pearsontechgroup.com

For sales outside of the U.S., please contact

International Sales

international@pearsoned.com

Acquisitions Editor Mark Taber	**Copy Editor** Keith Cline	**Technical Editor** John Coggeshall	**Designer** Chuti Prasertsith
Managing Editor Sandra Schroeder	**Indexer** Tim Wright	**Publishing Coordinator** Vanessa Evans	**Page Layout** Studio Galou
Project Editor Mandie Frank	**Proofreader** Kathy Ruiz		

Table of Contents

About the Author

Christian Wenz is a professional phrasemonger, author, trainer, and consultant with a focus on web technologies. He has written or cowritten more than one hundred books. He frequently contributes articles to renowned IT magazines and speaks at developer conferences around the globe. Christian contributes to several PHP libraries and frameworks and other open source software. He holds university degrees in computer sciences and in business informatics and lives and works in Munich, Germany. He also is one of the authors of Zend's PHP 5 and PHP 5.3 certifications.

We Want to Hear from You!

As the reader of this book, *you* are our most important critic and commentator. We value your opinion and want to know what we're doing right, what we could do better, what areas you'd like to see us publish in, and any other words of wisdom you're willing to pass our way.

You can email or write directly to let us know what you did or didn't like about this book—as well as what we can do to make our books stronger.

Please note that we cannot help you with technical problems related to the topic of this book, and that due to the high volume of mail we receive, we might not be able to reply to every message.

When you write, please be sure to include this book's title and author as well as your name and contact information.

Email: feedback@developers-library.info

Mail: Reader Feedback
                Addison-Wesley Developer's Library
                800 East 96th Street
                Indianapolis, IN 46240 USA

Reader Services

Visit our Web site and register this book at informit.com/register for convenient access to any updates, downloads, or errata that might be available for this book.

Introduction

Some time ago, my favorite development editor, Damon Jordan, sent me an email and closed it with *"Ich möchte eine Föhnwelle,"* which means "I'd like a blow wave." Unfortunately, I didn't know what either a *Föhnwelle* or a blow wave was, so I declined. He then told me he had found this sentence in a German phrasebook he recently bought.

I was interested and had a look at some German phrasebooks. I think they are great tools to get around in a foreign country, although I personally think that some of the phrases offered just don't make sense. For instance, in one phrasebook, I found a series of pickup lines, including the ingenious "You have a beautiful personality," something that didn't work for me either in English, in German, or in any other language! Some coital guidance could also result in other problems—you either have to remember all the things to say while you are at it, or you have to hold the phrasebook in your free hand. And, finally, "Blow waves are as dead as a pet rock," just to use another phrase.

Anyway, we were discussing phrasebooks a bit, and Damon said that he wanted to do a book series on phrasebooks. He also mentioned that he would like to team up with his and my favorite acquisitions editor, Shelley Johnston, so I was in.

While working on a concept, we found some differences between a language phrasebook and an IT phrasebook. For instance, a language phrasebook just contrasts the same sentence in two languages. However, this is not always helpful. What if you want to change the phrase a bit, for instance if you want an en vogue blow wave (an oxymoron, one might say)?

So, we tried to create a concept that contains a lot of phrases, but all of them with good explanations so that it is easy to change the code and adapt it to one's needs. This, of course, makes the "foreign language" portions of a phrase a bit longer than the phrase itself, but we think that really helps when working with the book.

I also remember one famous Monty Python sketch in which someone uses a sabotaged dictionary, so that asking for directions results in getting roughed up. Therefore, it is vitally important to get a real explanation on what is going on within the phrase.

I then wrote a series concept and a sample chapter, and now, only a few months later, you hold the first phrasebook in your hands (one of many, we hope).

Something I really hate about reading computer books is when code samples are hacked into the word processor but never tested. To avoid this, every listing is also available for download at http://php.phrasebook.org/; the filename is part of the listing's caption. So every code sample does exist as a file and has actually been tested, unlike in some other books. Of course, it's an illusion that this book is 100 percent error free, although we have taken several steps to come very close to that mark. Any errata, if known, will be posted to that site, too.

Another thing I really dislike with some books is that they tend to be very OS dependent, which is really unnecessary for PHP. Some books were obviously only tested under Windows, some others only under Linux, but it is possible to make code relatively platform independent. We have invested a lot of effort in testing the code from this book on many server platforms, including Linux, Windows, Mac OS X, and Solaris. Therefore, the screenshots in this book are also taken from those platforms, so you will find a healthy mixture of systems (and browsers). Ideology can be expressed with many phrases, but you won't find any of them in this book. If something does run only on certain platforms (or PHP versions), it is noted in the text. Another phrase I promise you will not find in this book is anything that looks like `foo`, `bar`, `baz`, or any other proofs of very little imagination.

Of course, it is easy to find missing phrases in this book. PHP offers so much functionality that it is impossible to cover every aspect. Therefore, we had to select certain topics of interest—stuff that is relevant in a PHP programmer's everyday work. If you think, however, that something has really been overlooked, please let me know (but do also nominate something that should then be removed from upcoming editions of this book to make room for the new phrases). I am looking forward to getting your feedback.

And now, to quote a phrasebook once more: "*Bist du soweit? Da boxt der Papst.*" That is, "Are you ready? It's all happening there" (but literally, "There boxes the pope.")

Your personal phrasemonger,

Christian Wenz

Introduction for the Second Edition

When we worked on the concept of the Phrasebook series a few years ago, we were quite confident that the books planned for the first batch would do well. Looking back now, with a dozen books still out there, and quite a number of foreign-language translations, I can say we did *really* well. It also makes me personally quite proud that the pilot, the *PHP Phrasebook*, still stands the test of time, and I am happy to see this book quite often when I am visiting a customer's site.

However, PHP has progressed quite a bit in the past few years. PHP 4 has finally vanished, and although the promised PHP 6 never materialized, PHP versions 5.3 and 5.4 added many new features, a lot of them originally planned for the next major PHP update.

We took this opportunity to update the *PHP Phrasebook* to the latest developments in PHP. Because we got really stellar feedback for the original book, we tried to leave the setup and popular phrases intact, but we added dozens of new and updated phrases, highlighting many of the new possibilities of PHP 5.3 and 5.4. For the sake of backward compatibility, we always mention in which version of PHP a new feature has been introduced, and if possible, we provide code that does not necessarily require the latest and greatest, if we see it fit.

The name of the book changed a bit, as well. We covered many relevant databases in the first edition, and still do now; however, MySQL continues to be the de facto standard database for PHP development, and therefore it gets its own chapter and part of the book's title page.

I am indebted to the many readers who provided me with suggestions, errata, and general feedback. Of course, any kind of feedback for this edition of the book is greatly appreciated, as well. The Web site at http://php.phrasebook.org/ contains the code samples from this book, errata (as soon as I learn about them), and contact information. I am looking forward to hearing from you!

As with most books, this has been a team effort. Mark Taber, who oversaw the creation of the Phrasebook series back then, is still onboard and was the project manager for this edition. I still remember when we drafted the new edition during breakfast on one of the rare occasions when we actually met in person. (Next time I'll pay.) I was happy that my old friend John Coggeshall was kind enough to serve as a technical reviewer—and to save my reputation a few times. Also "thank you" to the team of wizards at Pearson who turn my manuscripts into professional books. And thanks to my family and friends who accept the odd hours my profession requires from time to time.

1

Manipulating Strings

Of all data types PHP supports, string data is probably the one most often used. One of the reasons for this is that, at some point, a string representation of something is needed when sending out something to the client.

PHP offers a vast number of functions suitable for strings, almost 100. In addition, regular expressions come in handy when looking for certain patterns in strings. In real life, however, only a fraction of these functions are actually used. Most of them deserve their loyal fan base, but some underestimated functions should get more attention. The phrases in this chapter offer a good mix of both: standard applications and rather unusual but very useful ways to work with strings.

Comparing Strings

```
strcmp($a, $b)
strcasecmp($a, $b)
```

```php
<?php
  $a = 'PHP';
  $b = 'php';
  echo 'strcmp(): ' . strcmp($a, $b) . '<br />';
  echo 'strcasecmp(): ' . strcasecmp($a, $b);
?>
```

Comparing Strings (compare.php)

Which outputs

```
strcmp(): -32
strcasecmp(): 0
```

Comparing strings seems like an easy task—use the == operator for implicit type conversion (so '1' == 1 returns true) or the === operator for type checking (so '1' === 1 returns false). However, the first method is rather flawed because the type conversions are not always turned into strings. For instance, 1 == 'ltwothree' returns true, too; both values are converted into integers. Therefore, === is the way to go.

However, PHP also offers functions that offer a bit more than just comparing strings and returning true or false. Instead, strcmp() returns a positive value when the string passed as the first parameter is greater than the second parameter and a negative value when it is smaller. If both strings are equal, strcmp() returns 0. If no case sensitivity is required, strcasecmp() comes into play. It works as strcmp(), but it does not distinguish between uppercase and lowercase letters.

These two functions can be used to sort arrays. You can find more information about custom array sorting in Chapter 2, "Working with Arrays."

Checking Usernames and Passwords

```php
<?php
  $user = (isset($_GET['user'])) ? $_GET['user'] : '';
  $pass = (isset($_GET['pass'])) ? $_GET['pass'] : '';

  if (
    (strtolower($user) === 'damon' && $pass ===
➥'secret') ||
    (strtoupper($user) === 'SHELLEY' && $pass ===
➥'verysecret') ||
    (strcasecmp($user, 'Christian') == 0 &&
➥strcmp($pass, 'topsecret') == 0)
  ) {
    echo 'Login successful.';
  } else {
    echo 'Login failed.';
  }
?>
```

Validating Logins by Comparing Strings (comparelogin.php)

When validating a username and a password (for example, in a script that backs an HTML login form), two things seem to form a de facto standard on the Web:

- The password is always case sensitive. It has to be provided exactly the same way it was set.
- The username, however, is not case sensitive.

Therefore, a username has to be compared without considering case sensitivity. This can be done either by using strcasecmp()—see the previous phrase—or by first converting both the provided password and the real password into lowercase letters (or uppercase letters). This is done by the functions strtolower() or strtoupper(). The preceding code shows an example, using strcmp()/strcasecmp() and also the compare operator ===.

Depending on the data provided in the uniform resource locator (URL) of the call to the script, the login either fails or succeeds. For instance, the following URL successfully logs in the user. (You have to change the *servername* portion.)

```
http://servername/comparelogin.php
➥?user=cHRISTIAN&&pass=topsecret
```

In contrast, the following login does fail:

```
http://servername/comparelogin.php
➥?user=Christian&&pass=TopSecret
```

NOTE: Of course, providing usernames and passwords via GET is a very bad idea; POST is preferred. (See Chapter 4, "Interacting with Web Forms," for more details on form data.) However, for testing purposes, this chapter's code uses GET.

Converting Strings into HTML

```
htmlspecialchars($input)
htmlentities($input)
```

```php
<?php
  $input = '<script>alert("I have a bad
➥\'Föhnwelle\', ' .
          'therefore I crack
➥websites.");</script>';

  echo htmlspecialchars($input, ENT_QUOTES) . '<br
➥/>';
  echo htmlentities($input);
?>
```

Escaping Strings for HTML (htmlescape.php)

A commonly used Web attack is called Cross-Site Scripting (XSS). For example, a user enters some malicious data, such as JavaScript code, into a Web form; the Web page then at some point outputs this information verbatim, without proper escaping. Standard examples for this are Web guest books or discussion forms. People enter text for others to see it.

Here, it is important to remove certain HTML markup. To make a long story short: It is almost impossible to really catch all attempts to inject JavaScript into data. It's not only always done using the <script> tag, but also in other HTML elements, such as <img onabort="badCode()" />. Therefore, in most cases, all HTML must be removed.

The easiest way to do so is to call htmlspecialchars(); this converts the string into HTML, including replacement of all < and > characters with < and >. One notable exceptions are single quotes, which are not converted by default. However, when using the ENT_QUOTES constant as a second argument, single quotes are properly escaped, as well:

```
htmlspecialchars($input, ENT_QUOTES)
```

Another option is to call htmlentities(). This uses HTML entities for characters, if available. The preceding code shows the differences between these two methods. The German ö (o umlaut) is not converted by htmlspecialchars(); however, htmlentities() replaces it with its entity ö.

The use of htmlspecialchars() and htmlentities() just outputs what the user entered in the browser. So if the user enters HTML markup, this very markup is shown. Thus, htmlspecialchars() and htmlentities() please the browser but might not please the user.

NOTE: If you want to prepare strings to be used within URLs, you have to use urlencode() to properly encode special characters such as the space character that can be used in URLs.

However, the function strip_tags() does completely get rid of all HTML elements. If you just want to keep some elements (for example, some limited formatting functionalities with <b> and <i> and <br /> tags), you provide a list of allowed values in the second parameter for strip_tags(). The following script shows this; Figure 1.1 depicts its output. As you can see, all unwanted HTML tags have been removed; however, its contents are still there:

```php
<?php
  $input = 'My parents <i>hate</i> me, <br />' .
    'therefore I <b>crack</b> websites. ' .
    '<script>alert("Nice try!");</script>' .
    '<img src="explicit.jpg" />';

  echo strip_tags($input, '<b><br><i>');
?>
```

Figure 1.1 Some HTML tags were stripped, but not all.

Using Line Breaks

```php
<?php
  $input = "One\nTwo\r\nThree";
  echo nl2br($input);
?>
```

*Adding
 Elements at Every Line Break (nl2br.php)*

How can a line break be used within HTML? That's easy: with the
 HTML element. However, what if there is data with \n or \r\n line breaks? Search and replace comes to mind; however, it is much easier to use a built-in PHP function: nl2br(). This parses a string and converts all line breaks to <br /> elements, as the preceding script shows.

As you can see, the line breaks are still there, but the <br /> elements were added.

Encrypting Strings

```
$encpass = '$1$FK3.qn2.$Si5KhnprsRb.N.SEF4GMW0';
```

```php
<?php
  $pass = (isset($_GET['pass'])) ? $_GET['pass'] : '';
  $encpass = '$1$FK3.qn2.$Si5KhnprsRb.N.SEF4GMW0';

  if (crypt($pass, $encpass) === $encpass) {
    echo 'Login successful.';
  } else {
    echo 'Login failed.';
  }
?>
```

Checking Logins Using an Encrypted Password (crypt.php)

Passwords should never be stored verbatim in a database, but should instead be stored in an encrypted way. Some databases internally offer encryption; for all the others,

PHP is there to help. The `crypt()` function encrypts a string using Data Encryption Standard (DES). This is a one-way encryption, so there is no way back. Also, subsequent calls to `crypt()` result in different results.

For instance, the string `'TopSecret'` is encrypted into `$1$FK3.qn2.$Si5KhnprsRb.N.SEF4GMWO` (and also `$1$m61.1i2.$OplJ3EHwkIxycnyePplFz0` and `$1$9S3.c/3.$5l01Bm4v3cnBNOb1AECil.`, but this example sticks with the first one). Checking whether a value corresponds to a result from calling `crypt()` can be done by calling `crypt()` again: `crypt($value, $encryptedValue)` must return `$encryptedValue`.

The preceding script checks whether a password provided via the URL matches the previous result of `crypt()`. Calling this script with the GET parameter `pass=TopSecret` succeeds in logging in; all other passwords fail.

NOTE: To provide more details: The second parameter to `crypt()` is the salt (initialization value) for encrypting the data. You can also use a salt when encrypting the original password. However, you do have to make sure that the salt values are unique; otherwise, the encryption is not secure. Therefore, do not use a custom salt value and let PHP do the work.

Be also advised, though, that DES encryption can be cracked in about 24 hours, so it's not bulletproof anymore. A more recent alternative is Advanced Encryption Standard (AES).

Checksumming Strings

```
md5()
sha1()
```

```php
<?php
  $pass = (isset($_GET['pass'])) ? $_GET['pass'] :
➥'';

  $md5pass = '6958b43cb096e036f872d65d6a4dc01b';
  $sha1pass =
➥'61c2feed11e0e53eb8e295ab8da78150be12f301';

  if (sha1($pass) === $sha1pass) {
    echo 'Login successful.';
  } else {
    echo 'Login failed.';
  }

// Alternatively, using MD5:
//  if (md5($pass) === $md5pass) {
//    echo 'Login successful.';
//  } else {
//    echo 'Login failed.';
//  }
?>
```

Checking Logins Using SHA1 and MD5 Hashes
(checksum.php)

PHP offers these two main functions for creating checksums:

- md5() calculates the MD5 hash of a string.
- sha1() calculates the SHA1 hash of a string.

Using crypt() with strings is similar to creating a checksum of something: It can be easily determined whether a string matches the checksum; however, it is not (easily) possible to re-create the original string from the checksum.

Two algorithms whose purpose is to do exactly this checksumming are Secure Hash Algorithm 1 (SHA1) and Message Digest Algorithm 5 (MD5). They create such a checksum, or *hash*. The main difference between these two algorithms and the one used in DES/crypt() is that the SHA1 or MD5 checksum of a string is always the same, so it is very easy to verify data. As Figure 1.2 shows, even the PHP distributions have a MD5 checksum mentioned on the Web site to validate the downloads.

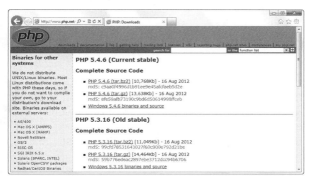

Figure 1.2 The PHP downloads page shows MD5 hashes of the PHP distributions.

Again, the goal is to validate a password the user provides using GET (which, as mentioned previously, is bad practice and only used for the sake of demonstration).

The correct password is, once again, `'TopSecret'` with the following hashes:

- `6958b43cb096e036f872d65d6a4dc01b` is the MD5 hash.

- `61c2feed11e0e53eb8e295ab8da78150be12f301` is the SHA1 hash.

From a security perspective, you should not rely on MD5 (because it can be broken with modern computers). SHA1 is not completely secure anymore, either, given the advances in hardware performance. You should consider additional safeguards:

- Before hashing a value, salt it—that is, prepend a known string, making it harder for attackers to crack it. That does not help against an attacker who uses brute force and tries almost all possible input combinations.

- Use `crypt()` with a more secure algorithm such as DES.

TIP: When calculating the MD5 or SHA1 hash of a file, no call to `file_get_contents()` or other file functions is required; PHP offers two functions that calculate the hashes of a file (and takes care of opening and reading in the file data):

- `md5_file()`
- `sha1_file()`

Extracting Substrings

substr()

```php
<?php
  $php = "PHP: Hypertext Preprocessor";
  echo substr($php, 15, 4); //returns "Prep"
?>
```

Extracting a Substring Using substr() (substr.php; excerpt)

The substr() function returns a part of a string. You provide a string and the position of the first character to be extracted. (Keep in mind that the first character has the index 0). From this character on, the rest of the string is returned. If you only want to return a part of it, provide the length in the third parameter. The preceding code shows substr() in action and extracts Prep from PHP: Hypertext Preprocessor.

TIP: If you want to count from the end of the string, use a negative value as the second parameter of substr():

```php
    echo substr($php, -12, 4);
```

If you provide a negative value for the third parameter of substr() (for example, –n,) the last n characters are not part of the substring.

```php
    echo substr($php, -12, -8);
```

All of these calls to substr() return Prep and are included in the complete code.

Protecting Email Addresses Using ASCII Codes

```
protectMail('email@address.xy')
```

```php
<?php
  function protectMail($s) {
    $result = '';
    $s = 'mailto:' . $s;
    for ($i = 0; $i < strlen($s); $i++) {
      $result .= '&#' . ord(substr($s, $i, 1)) . ';';
    }
    return $result;
  }

  echo '<a href="' .
    protectMail('email@address.xy') .
    '">Send mail</a>';
?>
```

Protecting Email Addresses (protectMail.php)

In the browser, you just see an email link, but the underlying HTML markup is indecipherable:

```
<a
href="&#109;&#97;&#105;&#108;&#116;&#111;&#58;
&#101;&#109;&#97;&#105;&#108;&#64;&#97;&#100;&#100;
&#114;&#101;&#115;&#115;&#46;&#120;&#121;">Send
mail</a>
```

However, take a look at Figure 1.3: The Web browser email address correctly decoded the email address, as shown in the status bar.

Figure 1.3   Machine beats man (when deciphering the email address).

Some special characters are difficult to use in strings because they are hard to enter using a keyboard. However, they all have an ASCII value. PHP offers two functions to deal with this:

- chr() converts the ASCII code into the corresponding character.

- ord() returns the ASCII code for a character.

This can be used to protect email addresses, for instance. Because spammers are writing software to search for certain patterns (email adresses) on Web pages, this might help keep spam low. The trick is to use HTML character codes for email addresses, making it much harder for spambots to find email data.

The preceding code takes an email address (in the format email@address.xy) as a parameter and returns mailto:email@address.xy—but converted into HTML entities. For instance, the m of mailto: has the ASCII code 109; therefore, `$#109;` stands for m. To do so, a `for` loop iterates through all characters in the string. In addition, the length of the string has to be determined, which can be done using `strlen()`. Then, a call to `ord()` calculates the ASCII code of each character, which is then used for the resulting HTML.

Of course, this does not offer bulletproof protection; you might consider using alternative ways to obscure the email address, including a syntax such as email at address dot xy.

Printing Strings, Variables, and Expressions Simultaneously

By using double quotation marks, printing a mixture of strings and variables is easy. However, when you also want to use expressions such as function calls, the standard way is to use lots of string concatenations:

```
echo 'The length of the string is ' . strlen($s) .
➥'!';
```

This is obviously getting rather complex when several expressions are involved.

A more convenient way is to use `printf()`. As parameters, you provide first a string with placeholders, and then the values for those placeholders. Table 1.1 shows which values are allowed for a placeholder.

Table 1.1   **Placeholders for** `printf()` **and Related Functions**

Placeholder	Description
%b	Integer value, binary representation is printed

Placeholder	Description
%c	Integer value, ASCII representation is printed
%d	Integer value, signed decimal value is printed
%e	Decimal value in scientific notation (1.2e+34)
%f	Float value, printed with respect to the locale settings
%F	Float value, printed without respect to the locale settings
%o	Integer value, octal representation is printed
%s	String value
%u	Integer value, unsigned decimal value is printed
%x	Integer value, hexadecimal representation with lowercase letters is printed
%X	Integer value, hexadecimal representation with uppercase letters is printed

The following shows how printf() makes the code a bit easier to read:

```php
<?php
  $a = 'PHP';
  $b = 'php';
  printf('strcmp(): %d<br />strcasecmp(): %d',
    strcmp($a, $b), strcasecmp($a, $b));
?>
```

PHP also supports several functions related to printf():

- sprintf() works like printf(), but returns the string and does not print it.
- vprintf() works like printf(), but expects the values for the placeholders in the string to be in the form of an array.
- vsprintf() is a mixture of sprintf() and vprintf(): The placeholder values are provided in an array, and the function returns the string but does not print it.

Scanning Formatted Strings

```
sscanf($date, '%d/%d/%d')
```

```php
<?php
  $date = '02/01/06';
  $values = sscanf($date, '%d/%d/%d');
  vprintf('Month: %d; Day: %d; Year: %d.', $values);
?>
```

Scanning Formatted Strings (sscanf.php)

Another function related to printf() is sscanf(). This one parses a string and tries to match it with a pattern that contains placeholders. The $input string contains a date and is scanned using the string '%d-%d-%d' with several placeholders, as shown in the preceding phrase. The function returns an array with all values for the matched placeholders. Then this array is passed to vprintf() to print it.

Alternatively, you can provide a list of variable names as additional parameters to sscanf(). Then the function writes the substrings that match the placeholders into these variables. The following code shows this:

```php
<?php
  $date = '02/01/06';
  $values = sscanf($date, '%d/%d/%d', $m, $d, $y);
  echo "Month: $m; Day: $d; Year: $y.";
?>
```

Scanning Formatted Strings (sscanf-alternative.php)

Getting Detailed Information about Variables

`var_dump(false);`

The values of variables can be sent to the client using print() or echo(); however, this is sometimes problematic. Take Booleans, for instance. echo(true) prints 1, but echo(false) prints nothing. A much better way is to use var_dump(), a function that also prints the type of the variable. Therefore, this code returns the string bool(false).

This also works for objects and arrays, making var_dump() a must-have option for developers who like to debug without a debugger.

NOTE: A function related to var_dump() is var_export(). It works similarly; however, there are two differences:

- The return value of var_export() is PHP code; for instance, var_export(false) returns false.
- If the second parameter provided to var_export() is the Boolean true, the function does not print anything, but returns a string.

Searching in Strings

strops()

```
if (!strpos($string, $substring)) {
  echo 'No match found.'
}
```

When looking for substrings in strings, strpos() is used (and its counterpart strrpos(), which searches from the end of the string). The tricky thing about this function is that it returns the index of the first occurrence of the substring, or false otherwise. That means that the preceding code snippet is incorrect.

The preceding code snippet is incorrect because if $string happens to start with $substring, strpos() returns 0, which evaluates to false. Therefore, a comparison using === or !== must be used to take the data type into account. The following code shows how to correctly use strpos():

```
if (strpos($string, $substring) === false) {
  echo 'No match found.';
} else {
  echo 'Match found.';
}
```

Understanding Regular Expressions

Regular expressions are, to put it simply, patterns that can be matched with strings. Two kinds of regular expressions are available in PHP: POSIX regular expressions and PHP regular expressions. The former are deprecated, so we only cover the latter option: Perl-compatible regular expressions (PCRE).

PCRE are often said to be faster, and do offer more features. This functionality is enabled in PHP by default; however, if you compile PHP by yourself, you can deactivate PCRE using the switch -without-pcre-regex.

A pattern in a regular expression contains a string that can be searched for in a larger string. However, this can also be done (faster) using strpos(). The advantage of regular expressions is that some special features such as wildcards are available. Table 1.2 shows some special characters and their meaning.

Table 1.2   **Special Characters in Regular Expressions**

Special Character	Description	Example
^	Beginning of the string	^a means a string that starts with a.
$	End of the string	a$ means a string that ends with a.
?	0 or 1 times (refers to the previous character or expression)	ab? means a or ab.

Table 1.2   **Continued**

Special Character	Description	Example
*	0 or more times (refers to the previous character or expression)	ab* means a or ab or abb or ...
+	1 or more times (refers to the previous character or expression)	ab+ means ab or abb or abbb or ...
[...]	Alternative characters	PHP[45] means PHP4 or PHP5
- (used within square brackets)	PHP[3-5] means PHP3 or PHP4 or PHP5.	A sequence of values
^ (used within square brackets)	Matches anything but the following characters	[^A-C] means D or E or F or ...
|	Alternative patterns	PHP4|PHP5 means PHP4 or PHP5
(...)	Defines a subpattern	(a)(b) means ab, but with two subpatterns (a and b).
.	Any character	. means a, b, c, 0, 1, 2, $, ^, ...
{min, max}	Minimum and maximum number of occurrences; if either min or max is omitted, it means 0 or infinite	a{1,3} means a, aa or aaa. a{,3} means empty string, a, aa, or aaa. a{1,} means a, aaa, aaa, ...

Special Character	Description	Example
\	Escapes the following character	\. stands for period (.).

TIP: The de facto standard reference for regular expressions is the title *Mastering Regular Expressions*, by Jeffrey E. F. Friedl—a fun read.

Other special characters and expressions are available (for instance, a character that refers to a digit, \d).

Using Perl-Compatible Regular Expressions

`preg_match()`

```php
<?php
  $string = 'This site runs on PHP ' . phpversion();
  preg_match('/php ((\d)\.\d\.\d+)/i',
    $string, $matches);
  vprintf('Match: %s<br /> Version: %s; Major: %d.',
    $matches);
?>
```

Searching in Strings Using PCRE (preg_match.php)

Matching patterns in PCRE is done using preg_match() if only one occurrence is searched for, or preg_match_all() if multiple occurrences may exist. The syntax is as follows: first the pattern, then the string, and then the resulting array. However, for the pattern you need delimiters; most of the time slashes are used. After the delimiter, you can provide further instructions. Instruction g lets the search be done globally (for multiple matches), whereas instruction i deactivates case sensitivity.

The function preg_match_all() works exactly the same; however, the resulting array is a multidimensional one. Each entry in this array is an array of matches as it would have been returned by preg_match(). The following code shows this:

```php
<?php
  $string = 'This site runs on PHP ' . phpversion();
  preg_match_all('/php ((\d)\.\d\.\d+)/i',
    $string, $matches);
  vprintf('Match: %s<br /> Version: %s; Major: %d.',
    $matches);
?>
```

Finding Multiple Matches in Strings Using PCRE (preg_match_all.php)

Finding Tags with Regular Expressions

```
preg_match_all('/<.*?>/', $string, $matches);
```

```php
<?php
  $string = '<p>Sex, drugs and <b>PHP</b>.</p>';
  preg_match_all('/<.*?>/', $string, $matches);
  foreach ($matches[0] as $match) {
    echo htmlspecialchars("$match ");
  }
?>
```

Finding All Tags Using Nongreedy PCRE (non-greedy.php)

Which outputs:

```
<p> <b> </b> </p>
```

One advantage of PCRE or POSIX is that some special constructs are supported. For instance, usually regular expressions are matched greedily. Take, for instance, this regular expression:

```
<.*>
```

When trying to match this in the following string

```
<p>Sex, drugs and <b>PHP</b>.</p>
```

what do you get? You get the complete string. Of course, the pattern also matches on `<p>`, but regular expressions try to match as much as possible. Therefore, you usually have to do a clumsy workaround, such as `<[^]*>`. However, it can be done more easily. You can use the ? modifier after the * quantifier to activate nongreedy matching.

Validating Mandatory Input

```
function checkNotEmpty($s) {
  return (trim($s) !== '');
}
```

When validating form fields (see Chapter 4 for more about HTML forms), several checks can be done. However, you should test as little as possible. For instance, when recently trying to order concert tickets for a U.S. concert, I failed to complete the order because the form expected a U.S. telephone number, which I could not provide.

The best check is to check whether there is any input at all. However, what is considered to be *any input*? If someone enters just whitespace (that is, space characters and other nontext characters), is the form field filled out correctly?

The best way is to use trim() before checking whether there is anything inside the variable or expression. The function trim() removes all kinds of whitespace characters, including the space character, horizontal and vertical tabs, carriage returns, and line feeds. If, after that, the string is not equal to an empty string, the (mandatory) field has been filled out.

NOTE: The file check.php contains sample calls and all following calls to validation functions in the file check.inc.php.

Validating Numbers (and Other Data Types)

To find out whether any data is a number (or can be converted into a number), PHP offers several possibilities. First, the following helper functions check the data type of a variable:

- **is_array()**—Checks for array
- **is_bool()**—Checks for Boolean
- **is_float()**—Checks for float
- **is_int()**—Checks for integer
- **is_null()**—Checks for null
- **is_numeric()**—Checks for integers and floats
- **is_object()**—Checks for object
- **is_string()**—Checks for string

It is to be noted, however, that the numeric functions—is_float(), is_int(), and is_numeric()—also try to convert the data from their original type to the numeric type.

Another approach to convert data types is something borrowed from Java and other strongly typed C-style languages. Prefix the variable or expression with the desired data type in parentheses:

```
$numericVar = (int)$originalVar;
```

In this case, however, PHP really tries to convert at any cost. Therefore, (int)'3DoorsDown' returns 3, whereas is_numeric('3DoorsDown') returns false. In contrast, (int)'ThreeDoorsDown' returns 0.

Generally, is_numeric() (and is_int()/is_float()) seems to be the better alternative, whereas (int) returns an integer value even for illegal input. So, it's really a matter of the specific application at hand which method to choose.

The following code offers the best of both worlds. A given input is checked whether it is numeric with is_numeric(), and if so, it is converted into an integer using (int). Adaptions to support other (numeric) data types are trivial:

```
function getIntValue($s) {
  if (!is_numeric($s)) {
    return false;
  } else {
    return (int)$s;
  }
}
```

Generating Integer Values (check.inc.php; excerpt)

Validating Email Addresses

```
function checkEmail($s) {
  $lastDot = strrpos($s, '.');
  $ampersat = strrpos($s, '@');
  $length = strlen($s);
  return !(
    $lastDot === false ||
    $ampersat === false ||
    $length === false ||
    $lastDot - $ampersat < 3 ||
    $length - $lastDot < 3
  );
}
```

Validating Email Addresses (check.inc.php; excerpt)

Checking whether a string contains a valid email address is two things at once: very common and very complicated. The aforementioned book on regular expressions uses several pages to create a set of regular expressions to perform this task. If you are interested in this, take a look at http://examples.oreilly.com/regex/readme.html.

Validating email addresses is difficult because the rules for valid domain names differ drastically between countries. For instance, bn.com is valid, whereas bn.de is not (but db.de is). Also, did you know that username@[127.0.0.1] is a valid email address (if 127.0.0.1 is the IP address of the mail server)?

Therefore, the recommendation is to only check for the major elements of an email address: valid characters (an @ character) and a dot somewhere after that. It is impossible to be 100 percent sure with checking email addresses; if the test is too strict, the user just provides a fantasy email address. The only purpose of email checking is to provide assistance when an (unintentional) typo occurs.

Of course, this is also possible using regular expressions, but this is probably just slower. You should also be aware that the aforementioned code cannot detect every email address that is incorrect. Also watch out for the new international domains with special characters such as ä or é in it. Most regular expressions omit these, so you are much better off with the preceding code.

Search and Replace

preg_replace()

```php
<?php
  $string = '02/01/13';
  echo preg_replace(
    '#(\d{1,2})/(\d{1,2})/(\d{1,2})#',
    '$2/$1/$3',
    $string
  );
?>
```

Replacing Matches Using PCRE (preg_replace.php)

Searching within strings is one thing; replacing all occurrences with something else is completely different. This is relatively easy, though, when using regular expressions; you just have to know the function name: preg_replace()

Within the regular expression for the replace term, you can use references to subpatterns. The complete match is referred to by $0. Then count parentheses from inside to outside, from left to right: The contents of the first parentheses are referenced by $1, the second parentheses are accessed using $2, and so on.

With this in mind, the replacement can be done. In the example, a U.S. date (month/day/year) is converted to a U.K. date (day/month/year).

TIP: The regular expression in the preceding code does not use the / delimiter for the regular expression because the regular expression itself contains slashes that would then need escaping. However, by choosing another delimiter (for example, #), you can avoid the escaping of slashes.

If you have a static pattern, without any quantifiers or special characters, using str_replace() is almost always faster. The parameter order for this is: first the strings to search for; then the replacements; and, finally, the string where the search and replace will take place. You can provide strings or arrays of strings in the first two parameters. The following code removes all punctuation from the text:

```php
<?php
  $string = 'To be, or not to be; that\'s the
➥question?!';
  echo str_replace(
    array('.', ',', ':', ';', '!', '?'),
    '',
    $string
  );
?>
```

Replacing without Regular Expressions(str_replace.php)

The following code shows how to use an array with replacement characters.

```php
<?php
  $string = '<p>This is <span
➥class="acronym">HTML</span>!</p>';
  echo str_replace(
    array('<', '>', '"', '\'', '&'),
    array('&lt;', '&gt;', '&quot;', '&apos;',
➥'&amp;'),
    $string
  );
?>
```

Replacing without Regular Expressions(str_replace_multiple.php)

2

Working with Arrays

When simple variables are just not good enough, arrays come into play (or objects, but that's another topic). The array section in the PHP manual, available at http://php.net/array, lists approximately 80 functions that are helpful. Therefore, this book could be filled with array-related phrases alone. However, not all of these functions are really used often. Therefore, this chapter presents the most important problems you'll have to solve when working with arrays—and, of course, solutions for these problems.

There are two types of arrays. The names they are given differ sometimes, but usually arrays are distinguished between numeric arrays and associative arrays. The first type of array uses numeric keys, whereas the latter type can also use strings as keys.

Creating an array can be done in one of three ways:

- Using the `array()` statement

```
$a = array('I', 'II', 'III', 'IV');
```

- Successively adding values to an array using the variable name and square brackets

```
$a[] = 'I';
$a[] = 'II';
$a[] = 'III';
$a[] = 'IV';
```

- Using a new square brackets syntax introduced in PHP 5.4

```
$a = ['I', 'II', 'III', 'IV'];
```

The latter method is probably the most intuitive one for Web developers because JavaScript features a very similar syntax. For the sake of backward compatibility, we will still use the first option throughout this chapter.

When using associative arrays, the same three methods can be used; however, this time keys and values must be provided:

```
$a1 = array('one' => 'I', 'two' => 'II', 'three' =>
➥'III', 'four' => 'IV');
$a2['one'] = 'I';
$a2['two'] = 'II';
$a2['three'] = 'III';
$a2['four'] = 'IV';

$a1 = ['one' => 'I', 'two' => 'II', 'three' =>
➥'III', 'four' => 'IV'];
```

Arrays can also be nested, when an array element itself is an array:

```
$a = array(
  'Roman' =>
    array('one' => 'I', 'two' => 'II', 'three' =>
'III', 'four' => 'IV'),
  'Arabic' =>
    array('one' => '1', 'two' => '2', 'three' =>
➥'3', 'four' => '4')
);
```

Now, the Arabic representation of the number four can be accessed using $a['Arabic']['four'].

Of course, arrays are not only created within a script but can also come from other sources, including from HTML forms (see Chapter 5, "Interacting with Web Forms") and from cookies and sessions (see Chapter 6, "Remembering Users (Cookies and Sessions)"). But if the array is there, what's next? The following phrases give some pointers.

Accessing All Elements of Numeric Arrays

foreach ($a as $element)

```php
<?php
  $a = array('I', 'II', 'III', 'IV');
  foreach ($a as $element) {
    echo htmlspecialchars($element) . '<br />';
  }
?>
```

Looping through an Array with foreach (foreach-n.php)

Looping through numeric (or indexed) arrays can most easily be done using foreach because in each iteration of the loop, the current element in the array is automatically written in a variable, as shown in the preceding code.

Alternatively, a for loop can also be used. The first array element has the index 0; the number of array indices can be retrieved using the count() function:

```php
<?php
  $a = array('I', 'II', 'III', 'IV');
  for ($i = 0; $i < count($a); $i++) {
    echo htmlspecialchars($a[$i]) . '<br />';
  }
?>
```

Looping through an Array with for (for-n.php)

Both ways are equally good (or bad); though, usually, using foreach is the much more convenient way. However, there is a third possibility: The PHP function each() returns the current element in an array. The return value of each() is an array, in which you can access the value using the numeric index 1, or the string index 'value'. Using a while loop, the whole array can be traversed. The following code once again prints all elements in the array, this time using each():

```php
<?php
  $a = array('I', 'II', 'III', 'IV');
  while ($element = each($a)) {
    echo htmlspecialchars($element['value']) .
➡'<br />'; //or: $element[1]
  }
?>
```

Looping through an Array with each (each-n.php)

The output of the three listings is always the same, of course.

Accessing All Elements of Associative Arrays

```
foreach ($a as $key => $value)
```

```php
<?php
  $a = array('one' => 'I', 'two' => 'II', 'three' =>
➥'III', 'four' => 'IV');
  foreach ($a as $key => $value) {
    echo htmlspecialchars("$key: $value") . '<br
➥/>';
  }
?>
```

Looping through an Associative Array with foreach (foreach-a.php)

When using an associative array and wanting to access all data in it, the keys are also of relevance. For this, the foreach loop can also provide a variable name for the element's key, not only for its value.

Using count() is possible: count() returns the number of values in the array, not the number of elements. Looping through all array elements with for is not feasible. However, the combination of each() and while can be used, as shown in the following code. The important point is that the key name can be retrieved either using the index 0 or the string index 'key':

```php
<?php
  $a = array('one' => 'I', 'two' => 'II', 'three' =>
➡'III', 'four' => 'IV');
  while ($element = each($a)) {
    echo htmlspecialchars($element['key'] . ': ' .
➡$element['value']) . '<br />';
    //or: $element[0] / $element[1]
  }
?>
```

Looping through an Associative Array with each (each-a.php)

Accessing All Array Elements in Nested Arrays

```
print_r($a);
```

```php
<pre>
<?php
  $a = array(
    'Roman' =>
      array('one' => 'I', 'two' => 'II', 'three' =>
➡'III', 'four' => 'IV'),
    'Arabic' =>
      array('one' => '1', 'two' => '2', 'three' =>
➡'3', 'four' => '4')
  );
  print_r($a);
?>
</pre>
```

Printing a Nested Array with print_r (print_r.php)

Nested arrays can be printed really easily by using
print_r(). Take a look at the output of the listing in
Figure 2.1.

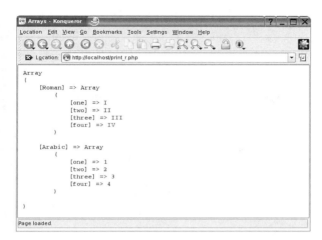

Figure 2.1   Printing array contents with `print_r()`

TIP: If you set the second parameter of `print_r()` to
`true`, the associative array's contents are not sent to
the client, but are returned from the function, so that
you can save this information in a variable and process
it further.

However, the output of the preceding code (see Figure
2.1) is hardly usable for more than debugging purposes.
Therefore, a clever way to access all data must be
found. A recursive function is a reasonable way to
achieve this. In this, all elements of an array are printed
out; the whole output is indented using the HTML
element `<blockquote>`. If the array element's value is an
array itself, however, the function calls itself recursively,
which leads to an additional level of indention.

Whether something is an array can be determined using the PHP function is_array(). Using this, the following code can be assembled; see Figure 2.2 for the result:

```php
<?php
  function printNestedArray($a) {
    echo '<blockquote>';
    foreach ($a as $key => $value) {
      echo htmlspecialchars("$key: ");
      if (is_array($value)) {
        printNestedArray($value);
      } else {
        echo htmlspecialchars($value) . '<br />';
      }
    }
    echo '</blockquote>';
  }

  $arr = array(
    'Roman' =>
      array('one' => 'I', 'two' => 'II', 'three' =>
'III', 'four' => 'IV'),
    'Arabic' =>
      array('one' => '1', 'two' => '2', 'three' =>
'3', 'four' => '4')
  );

  printNestedArray($arr);
?>
```

Printing a Nested Array Using a Recursive Function
(printNestedArray.php)

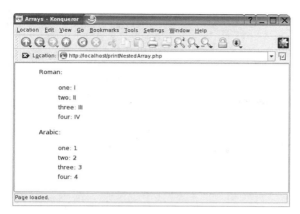

Figure 2.2 Printing array contents using a recursive function

Turning an Array into Variables

```
while (list($key, $value) = each($a))
```

```php
<?php
  $a = array('one' => 'I', 'two' => 'II', 'three' =>
'III', 'four' => 'IV');
  while (list($key, $value) = each($a)) {
    echo htmlspecialchars("$key: $value") . '<br
/>';
  }
?>
```

Looping through an Array with list() *and* each()
(each-list.php)

Whenever each() is used, the use of list() is a good idea. Within list(), you provide variable names for all values with numeric indices in the array that is returned by each(). This makes while/each() loops even easier to use, as the code shows. Within the parentheses, the variable names are provided.

TIP: If you are interested only in either the key or the value of the array, you can remove one of the two variables; just make sure that you keep the comma.

```
while (list(, $value) = each($a)) {
  echo htmlspecialchars("$value") . '<br />';
}
```

Converting Strings to Arrays

```
$a = explode(',', $csvdata);
```

```php
<?php
  $csvdata = 'Pearson Education,800 East 96th
➥Street,Indianapolis,Indiana,46240';
  $a = explode(',', $csvdata);
  $info = print_r($a, true);
  echo "<pre>$info</pre>";
?>
```

Turning a String into an Array (explode.php)

Sometimes, arrays are not used to store information; instead, a string is used. The single values are all within the string, but are separated by a special character. One example for this is the comma-separated values (CSV) format.

The PHP function explode() creates an array out of these values; you just have to provide the characters at which the string needs to be split. The browser then shows this output:

```
Array
(
    [0] => Pearson Education
    [1] => 800 East 96th Street
    [2] => Indianapolis
    [3] => Indiana
    [4] => 46240
)
```

Converting Arrays to Strings

```
$address = implode('<br />', $data);
```

```php
<?php
  $data = array(
    'Pearson Education',
    '800 East 96th Street',
    'Indianapolis',
    'Indiana',
    '46240'
  );
  $address = implode('<br />', $data);
  echo $address;
?>
```

Turning an Array into a String (implode.php)

The way back (that is, making a string representation out of the elements in an array) can be done using implode(). Again, two parameters are required: the separation elements, then the array. The order is quite unusual, yet important.

So, PHP joins the elements of the array, using the

 HTML element. Therefore, in the browser,
each array's elements stay at its own line.

Sorting Arrays Alphabetically

```
sort($a, SORT_NUMERIC);
sort($a, SORT_STRING);
```

```
<pre>
<?php
  $a = array('4', 31, '222', 1345);
  sort($a, SORT_NUMERIC);
  print_r($a);
  sort($a, SORT_STRING);
  print_r($a);
?>
</pre>
```

Sorting an Array (`sort.php`*)*

Numeric arrays can be sorted rather easily by using
sort(). However, a problem exists if the array contains
both numeric and string values (for instance, "2" >
"10" but 2 < 10). Therefore, the sorting can be tweaked
so that a special data type is used for comparing elements when sorting:

- SORT_NUMERIC sorts elements as numbers.
- SORT_REGULAR sorts elements according to their data
  type (standard behavior).
- SORT_STRING sorts elements as strings.

Here is the output of the preceding listing:

```
Array
(
```

```
    [0] => 4
    [1] => 31
    [2] => 222
    [3] => 1345
)
Array
(
    [0] => 1345
    [1] => 222
    [2] => 31
    [3] => 4
)
```

NOTE: If you want to sort the elements of the array in reverse order, use rsort() (*r* for reverse). The same optional second parameters are allowed that can be used with sort().

Sorting Associative Arrays Alphabetically

```
ksort($a);
asort($a);
```

```
<pre>
<?php
  $a = array('one' => 'I', 'two' => 'II', 'three' =>
➥'III', 'four' => 'IV');
  ksort($a);
  print_r($a);
  asort($a);
  print_r($a);
?>
</pre>
```

Sorting an Associative Array (sort_a.php)

Sorting associative arrays can be done in one of several ways:

- Sort by keys, leave key-value association intact: Use ksort().

- Sort by keys in reverse order, leave key-value association intact: Use krsort().

- Sort by values, leave key-value association intact: Use asort().

- Sort by values in reverse order, leave key-value association intact: Use arsort().

The preceding code shows these functions in action; Figure 2.3 shows the result.

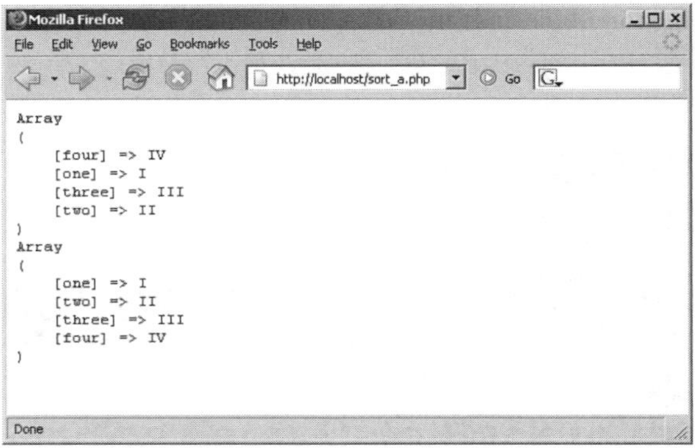

Figure 2.3   Sorting associative arrays

NOTE: Trying to use sort() or rsort() with associative arrays works, but the keys are then all lost.

Sorting Nested Arrays

```
function sortNestedArray(&$a) {
  sort($a);
  for ($i = 0; $i < count($a); $i++) {
    if (is_array($a[$i])) {
      sortNestedArray($a[$i]);
    }
  }
}
```

```php
<pre>
<?php
  function sortNestedArray(&$a) {
    sort($a);
    for ($i = 0; $i < count($a); $i++) {
      if (is_array($a[$i])) {
        sortNestedArray($a[$i]);
      }
    }
  }

  $arr = array(
    'French',
    'Spanish',
    array('British English', 'American English'),
    'Portuguese',
    array('Schwitzerdütsch', 'Deutsch'),
    'Italian'
  );
  sortNestedArray($arr);
  print_r($arr);
?>
</pre>
```

Sorting a Nested Array Using a Recursive Function
(sortNestedArray.php)

The standard sorting functions of PHP do not traverse nested arrays when performing their operations. However, if you use a recursive function, you can code this in just a few lines.

The goal is to sort an array that is nested but consists only of numeric subarrays so that only numeric (and, therefore, useless) keys are used.

The idea is the following: Calling sort() does sort the array, but leaves out all subarrays. Therefore, for all elements that are arrays, the sorting function is called again, recursively. The preceding code shows this concept; Figure 2.4 shows the result for a sample array.

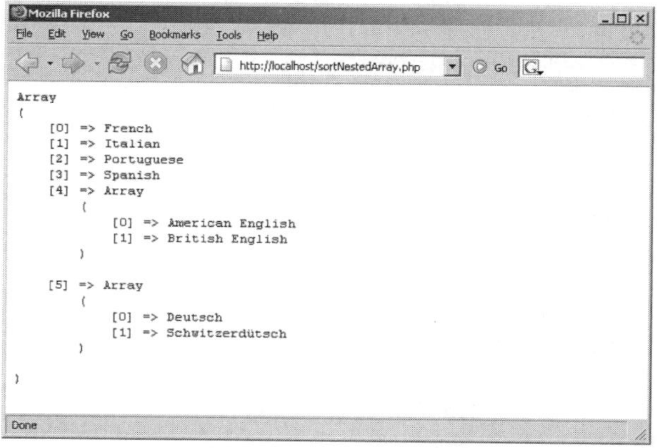

Figure 2.4   Sorting nested arrays

NOTE: The PHP function array_multisort() is an alternative way to sort arrays with more than one dimension.

Sorting Nested Associative Arrays

```
foreach ($a as $key => $value) {
  if (is_array($value)) {
    sortNestedArrayAssoc($value);
  }
}
```

```
<pre>
<?php
  function sortNestedArrayAssoc($a) {
    ksort($a);
    foreach ($a as $key => $value) {
      if (is_array($value)) {
        sortNestedArrayAssoc($value);
      }
    }
  }

  $arr = array(
    'Roman' =>
      array('one' => 'I', 'two' => 'II', 'three' =>
➥'III', 'four' => 'IV'),
    'Arabic' =>
      array('one' => '1', 'two' => '2', 'three' =>
➥'3', 'four' => '4')
  );
  sortNestedArrayAssoc(&$arr);
  print_r($arr);
?>
</pre>
```

*Sorting an Associative Nested Array Using a Recursive Function
(sortNestedArrayAssoc.php)*

If an associative nested array is to be sorted, two things
have to be changed in comparison to the previous

phrase that sorted a numeric (but nested) array. First, the array has to be sorted using ksort(), not sort(). Furthermore, the recursive sorting has to be applied to the right variable, the array element that itself is an array. Make sure that this is passed via reference so that the changes are applied back to the value:

```
foreach ($a as $key => &$value) {
  if (is_array($value)) {
    sortNestedArrayAssoc($value);
  }
}
```

Figure 2.5 shows the result of the code at the beginning of this phrase.

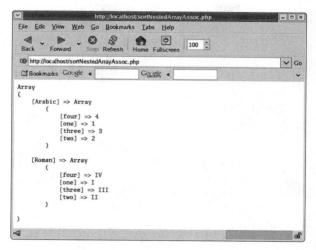

Figure 2.5   Sorting nested, associative arrays

Sorting IP Addresses (as a Human Would)

```
natsort($a);
```

```php
<?php
  $a = array('100.200.300.400', '100.50.60.70',
➥'100.8.9.0');
  natsort($a);
  echo implode(' < ', $a);
?>
```

Sorting IP Addresses Using a Natural String Order String Comparison (natsort.php)

Sorting IP addresses with `sort()` does not really work because if sorting as strings, `'100.200.300.400'` (which intentionally is an invalid IP) is less than `'50.60.70.80'`. In addition, there are more than just digits within the string, so a numeric sorting does not work.

What is needed in this case is a so-called natural sorting, something that has been implemented by Martin Pool's Natural Order String Comparison project at http://sourcefrog.net/projects/natsort/. In PHP's `natcasesort()` function, this algorithm is used. According to the description, it sorts "as a human would." When case sensitivity is an issue, `natsort()` can be used. The preceding code shows the latter function.

NOTE: Internally, `natsort()` uses `strnatcmp()` (and `natcasesort()` uses `strnatcasecmp()`), which does a "natural" comparison of two strings. By calling this function a number of times, the array elements are brought into the correct order.

Sorting Anything

```php
<?php
  function compare($a, $b) {
    return $a - $b;
  }

  $a = array(4, 1345, 31, 222);
  usort($a, 'compare');
  echo implode(' < ', $a);
?>
```

If you do not want to limit yourself to the standard sorting functionality offered by PHP, you can write your own sorting algorithm. Internally, PHP uses the Quicksort algorithm to sort values in an array. For this to work, PHP has to know whether two values are equal; in the latter case, PHP needs to find out which value is greater. So, to implement a custom sort, all that is required is a function that takes two parameters and returns:

- A negative value if the first parameter is smaller than the second parameter
- 0 if both parameters are equal
- A positive value if the second parameter is smaller than the first parameter

The name of this function must be passed to usort()—as a string—or, if you are using at least PHP 5.3, you can also rely on an anonymous function similar to JavaScript. The rest of the work is done by PHP, as shown in the code. The comparison function used there is a very simple way to do a numeric sorting. By substracting the two values, the function returns the desired values: A positive number if the first parameter is larger than the second one, 0 if both parameters are equal, and a negative number otherwise.

Sorting with Foreign Languages

```php
<?php
  function compare($a, $b) {
    if ($a == $b) {
      return 0;
    } else {
      for ($i = 0; $i < min(strlen($a), strlen($b));
➥$i++) {
        $cmp = compareChar(substr($a, $i, 1),
➥substr($b, $i, 1));
        if ($cmp != 0) {
          return $cmp;
        }
      }
      return (strlen($a) > strlen($b)) ? 1 : 0;
    }
  }

  function compareChar($a, $b) {
    // ...
  }

  $a = array('Frédéric', 'Froni', 'Frans');
  usort($a, 'compare');
  echo implode(' < ', $a);
?>
```

*Sorting an Array with Language-Specific Characters
(languagesort.php; excerpt)*

Sorting works well, as long as only the standard ASCII
characters are involved. However, as soon as special language characters come into play, the sorting yields an
undesirable effect. For instance, calling sort() on an
array with the values 'Frans', 'Frédéric', and 'Froni'
puts 'Frédéric' last because the é character has a much
larger charcode than o.

For this special case, PHP offers no special sorting method; however, you can use strnatcmp()to emulate this behavior. The idea is to define a new order for some special characters; in the comparison function, you then use this to find out which character is "larger" and which is "smaller."

You first need a function that can sort single characters:

```
function compareChar($a, $b) {
    $characters =
'AÀÁÄBCÇDEÈÉFGHIÌÍJKLMNOÒÓÖPQRSTUÙÚÜVWXYZ';
    $characters .=  'aàáäbcçdeèéfghiìíjklm
➥noòóöpqrstuùúüvwxyz';
    $pos_a = strpos($characters, $a);
    $pos_b = strpos($characters, $b);
    if ($pos_a === false) {
      if ($pos_b === false) {
        return 0;
      } else {
        return 1;
      }
    } elseif ($pos_b === false) {
      return -1;
    } else {
      return $pos_a - $pos_b;
    }
  }
```

Then, the main sorting function calls compareChar(), character for character, until a difference is found. If no difference is found, the longer string is considered to be the "greater" one. If both strings are identical, 0 is returned. The code at the beginning of this phrase shows the compare function. The result of this code is, as desired, Frans < Frédéric < Froni.

Starting with PHP 5.3, the ext/intl extension provides a mechanism for natural language sorting, as well. If the extension is installed (which may additionally require the ICU library set from http://site.icu-project.org/), you first need to create a so-called collator, which expects a locale (for instance, en_US, en_CA, en_GB, fr_FR, or de_AT). Then, you can call the sort() and asort() methods, which work analogously to their PHP counterparts but take the locale information into account:

```php
$a = array('Frédéric', 'Froni', 'Frans');
$coll = new Collator('fr_FR');
$coll->sort($a);
echo implode(' < ', $a);
```

Sorting an Array with Locale Information (collator.php)

Applying an Effect to All Array Elements

```php
$a = array_map('sanitize', $a);
```

```php
<?php
  function sanitize($s) {
    return htmlspecialchars($s);
  }

  $a = array('harmless', '<bad>', '>>click
➥here!<<');
  $a = array_map('sanitize', $a);
  echo implode(' ', $a);
?>
```

Applying htmlspecialchars() to All Elements of an Array (array_map.php)

Sometimes, data in an array has to be preprocessed before it can be used. In Chapter 4, you will see how data coming from the user via HTML forms can be sanitized before it is used. To do so, every array element must be touched.

However, it is not required that you do a cumbersome for/foreach/while loop; PHP offers built-in functionality for this. The first possibility is to use array_map(). This takes an array (second parameter) and submits every element in that array to a callback function (first parameter, as a string, an array, or an anonymous function, as you can see below). At the end, the array is returned, with all of the elements replaced by the associated return values of the callback function.

In the preceding listing, all values in the array are converted into HTML using htmlspecialchars().

NOTE: Starting with PHP 5.3, you may use inline anonymous functions whenever a callback is expected by a PHP function. So, the previous code could be cleaned up a bit like this:

```php
<?php
  $a = array('harmless', '<bad>', '>>click
➥here!<<');
  $a = array_map(
    function sanitize($s) {
      return htmlspecialchars($s);
    }.
    $a);
  echo implode(' ', $a);
?>
```

Applying htmlspecialchars() *to All Elements of an Array, Using an Anonymous Function (array_map_anon.php)*

If the array turns out to be a nested one, however, the tactic has to be changed a little. Then you can use a recursive function. If an array element is a string, it is HTML encoded. If it's an array, the recursive function calls itself on that array. The following code implements this, and Figure 2.6 shows the result:

```php
<?php
  function sanitize_recursive($s) {
    if (is_array($s)) {
      return(array_map('sanitize_recursive', $s));
    } else {
      return htmlspecialchars($s);
    }
  }

  $a = array(
    'harmless' =>
      array('no', 'problem'),
    'harmful' =>
      array('<bad>', '-> <worse> <<-')
  );

  $a = sanitize_recursive($a);
  echo '<pre>' . print_r($a, true) . '</pre>';
?>
```

Recursively Applying htmlspecialchars() *to All Elements of a Nested Array (array_map_recursive.php)*

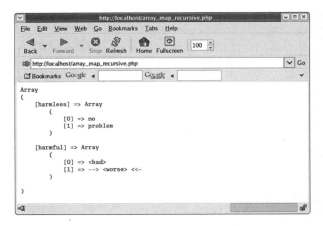

Figure 2.6   The nested arrays have been HTML-encoded.

Another function that behaves similarly is array_walk().
This one also applies a function to every element of an
array; however, it also allows you to provide a parameter for this function call. In the following code, this is
used to print out all elements of an array. A parameter
is passed—a counter. Because it is passed by reference,
increasing this counter by one within the function
leads to a sequence of numbers:

```php
<?php
  function printElement($s, &$i) {
    printf('%d: %s<br />', $i,
➥htmlspecialchars($s));
    $i++;
  }

  $i = 1;
  $a = array('one', 'two', 'three', 'four');
```

```
  $a = array_walk($a, 'printElement', $i);
?>
```

Printing Array Elements Using array_walk() *and a Counter
Passed by Reference (array_walk.php)*

Running the preceding code shows the following:

```
0: one
1: two
2: three
3: four
```

Filtering Arrays

```
array_filter($values, 'checkMail')
```

```php
<?php
  function checkMail($s) {
    // ...
  }

  $values = array(
    'valid@email.tld',
    'invalid@email',
    'also@i.nvalid',
    'also@val.id'
  );
  echo implode(', ', array_filter($values,
➥'checkMail'));
?>
```

Filtering Valid Email Addresses (array_filter.php)

Imagine you get a bunch of values—from an HTML form, a file, or a database—and want to select which of these values are actually usable and which are not. You could again call for, foreach, or while and find out what is interesting, or you can let PHP do most of the work. In the latter case, get acquainted with the function array_filter(). This one takes two parameters: first, the array to be filtered; and second, a function name (as a string) that checks whether an array element is good. This validation function returns true upon success and false otherwise. The following is a very simple validation function for email addresses; see Chapter 1, "Manipulating Strings," for a much better one:

```
function checkMail($s) {
  $ampersand = strpos($s, '@');
  $lastDot = strrpos($s, '.');
  return ($ampersand !== false &&
          $lastDot !== false &&
          $lastDot - $ampersand >= 3);
}
```

Now, the code at the beginning of this phrase calls array_filter() so that only (syntactically) valid email addresses are left.

As you would expect, the code just prints out the two valid email addresses.

Getting Random Elements Out of Arrays

```php
array_rand($numbers, 6)
```

```php
<?php
  for ($i = 1; $i <= 49; $i++) {
    $numbers[] = $i;
  }
  // we could use range() instead, too

  echo implode(' ', array_rand($numbers, 6));
?>
```

Picking Random Elements Out of an Array (array_rand.php)

With array_rand(), one or more random elements out of an array are determined by random. This can, for instance, be used to draw some lucky numbers. For instance, the German lottery draws 6 numbers out of 49. The preceding code implements this drawing using PHP and array_rand(); see Figure 2.7 for its output. The first parameter for this function is the array; the second (optional) one is the number of elements to be returned.

NOTE: If you do not want to pick random elements but want to randomize the order of elements in the array (for example, when shuffling a deck of cards), use the shuffle() function.

Figure 2.7   Lucky numbers with PHP

Making Objects Behave Like Arrays

```
class MyArray implements ArrayAccess, Countable

<?php
  class MyArray implements ArrayAccess, Countable {
      private $_data = array();

      /* ArrayAccess interface */
      public function offsetSet($offset, $value) {
        $this->_data[$offset] = $value;
      }

      public function offsetExists($offset) {
        return isset($this->_data[$offset]);
      }

      public function offsetUnset($offset) {
        unset($this->_data[$offset]);
      }
```

```
    public function offsetGet($offset) {
      //return (isset($this->_data[$offset])) ?
➥$this->_data[$offset] : null;
      return ($this->offsetExists($offset)) ?
➥$this->_data[$offset] : null;
    }

    /* Countable Interface */
    public function count() {
      return count($this->_data);
    }

  }

  $a = new MyArray();
  $a[0] = 'I';
  $a[1] = 'II';
  $a[2] = 'III';
  $a[3] = 'IV';
  for ($i = 0; $i < count($a); $i++) {
    printf('<p>%s</p>', htmlspecialchars($a[$i]));
  }
?>
```

Using an Object Like an Array with SPL (splArray.php)

SPL, the Standard PHP Library, is one of the most underrated features of PHP. It basically offers a huge set of interfaces. If you create a class using one of those interfaces, you might use standard PHP functions with your class. The documentation at http://php.net/spl is not always as detailed as you would expect, but it does give you some great pointers as to what is possible.

As a simple example, we will create a class (you can find more about various aspects of object-oriented programming [OOP] in Chapter 4) that implements two interfaces:

- **ArrayAccess**—Allows accessing individual elements within the object's collection (in our code, a simple array)

- **Countable**—Allows calling count() on an object instance

If you want full array support, you need to implement additional interfaces, including Iterable (for iterator support; for example, via foreach) and some more. The ArrayObject interface aggregates several of the required interfaces, which in turn could even allow advanced features like user-defined sorting.

3

Date and Time

Most of the time, the date and time functionalities of PHP 5 are used for printing out the current date and time—to pretend that the Web page is up-to-date. (You would be surprised how many larger Web sites actually use this.) But apart from that, working with date and time in PHP offers many other possibilities, most of which you will find in this chapter. As of PHP version 5.2, the completely new DateTime extension was added to the PHP core. Of course, this does not affect existing functionality, which continues to work fine, but there are some new features, some of them also covered in this chapter.

First, though, it seems appropriate to take a look at the PHP function that is probably used the most for working with dates: date(). This function can take the current date (or an arbitrary one) and extract some information about it (for example, the day, whether it's a.m. or p.m., and what time it is according to the rather failed marketing stunt Swatch Internet Time). To do so, you call date() and provide a string as the first parameter. This string may now contain a list of formatting symbols that are shown in Table 3.1. (The PHP manual contains a list with more examples at http://php.net/date.) Each symbol is replaced by the associated date/time value.

Table 3.1   **Formatting Symbols for** date()

Symbol	Description
a	am or pm
A	AM or PM
B	Swatch Internet Time (between 000 and 999)
c	Date in ISO 8601 format
d	Day of month (from 01 to 31)
D	Day of week (from Mon to Sun)
F	Month (from January to December)
g	Hour (from 1 to 12)
G	Hour (from 0 to 23)
h	Hour (from 01 to 12)
H	Hour (from 00 to 23)
i	Minutes (from 00 to 59)
I	Whether date is in DST (1) or not (0)
j	Day of month (between 1 and 31)
l	Day of month (from Sunday to Saturday)
L	Whether date is in a leap year (1) or not (0)
m	Month (from 01 to 12)
M	Month (from Jan to Dec)
n	Month (from 1 to 12)
O	Difference to GMT (for example, +0100 for 1 hour ahead)
r	Date in RFC 2822 format
s	Seconds (from 00 to 59)
S	Ordinal suffix for the day of month (st, nr, td, th)
t	Number of days in the provided month (from 28 to 31)

Symbol	Description
T	Time zone of server (for example, CET)
U	Epoch value (seconds since January 1st, 1970, midnight GMT)
w	Day of week (from 0 [Sunday] to 6 [Saturday])
W	Week number (according to ISO 8601, from 1 to 53)
y	Year (2 digits)
Y	Year (4 digits)
z	Day of year (from 0 to 365)
Z	Time zone difference to UTC (in seconds)

NOTE: Almost all the formatting symbols shown in Table 3.1 are available since PHP 3. There are only two exceptions: Using W for determining the week number of a date was added in PHP 4.1.0, and using c for retrieving the ISO 8601 representation for a date (for example, 2006-06-30T12:34:56+01:00) came in PHP 5.

The function date() is very powerful and offers a broad range of ways to use it. However, especially if you have localized content, you need some good phrases. In this chapter, you will find many of them.

The newer way of date and time handling in PHP uses, among other classes, DateTime. We use this class and some related ones in selected phrases in this chapter, as well.

PHP's date and time features have their own section in the PHP manual. You can find more information about DateTime and friends at http://php.net/datetime.

Using Text within `date()`

```php
<?php
  echo date('\To\d\a\y \i\s \t\he jS \d\a\y of F');
?>
```

Suppose you want to output the current date (or a specific date) and use custom strings in it. The code could look like a mess if you are trying it like this:

```php
<?php
  echo 'Today is the ' . date('jS') . ' day of the
➥month ' . date('F');
?>
```

The output of this script is something like this, depending on the current date:

```
Today is the 3rd day of the month May
```

The behavior of `date()` is as follows: All characters within the first parameter that bear a special meaning (for example, formatting symbols) get replaced by the appropriate values. All other characters, however, remain unchanged. If a character is escaped using the backslash character (\), it is returned verbatim. So, the code at the beginning of this phrase shows a new version of the code that uses only one call to `date()`.

NOTE: If you are using double quotes rather than single quotes, you might get into trouble when escaping certain characters within `date()`. In the previous example, escaping the n would be done with \n, which (within double quotes) gets replaced by the newline character.

Formatting DateTime Objects

The new date- and time-handling approach introduced in PHP 5.2 uses the DateTime class to represent a date value. There are several ways to create a class instance, but probably the most convenient one is to provide a date in a given format and tell PHP in turn which format you have been using. The formatting symbols are those from Table 3.1. Here is an example:

```php
$d = DateTime::createFromFormat('d.m.Y', '21.11.2012');
```

The variable $d now holds a date that represents the 21st of November, 2012.

After we have acquired such a date and worked with it (see some of the other phrases in this chapter), we can format the date as a string, using the same formatting characters as before, plus the format() method:

```php
echo $d->format('Y-m-d');
```

NOTE: Apart from the object-oriented programming (OOP) application programming interface (API), PHP's DateTime features are also available using a procedural interface. The preceding lines of code could also look like this— although we prefer the OOP syntax in this chapter:

```php
$d = date_create_from_format('d.m.Y', '10.11.2012');
echo date_format($d, 'Y-m-d');
```

Automatically Localizing Dates

```php
<?php
  setlocale(LC_TIME, 'en_US');
  echo strftime('In (American) English: %c<br />');
  setlocale(LC_TIME, 'en_GB');
```

```
  echo strftime('In (British) English: %c<br />');
  setlocale(LC_TIME, 'de_DE');
  echo strftime('Auf Deutsch: %c<br />');
  setlocale(LC_TIME, 'fr_FR');
  echo strftime('En Français: %c');
?>
```

The PHP function strftime() formats a date/time value according to the system's locale (for example, to the Web server's local settings). Generally, the language of the system is automatically used. However, this can be overridden using setlocale().

The function strftime() expects a format string (as does date()) in which it accepts a large number of special symbols. Table 3.2 contains a full list.

Table 3.2   Formatting Symbols for strftime()

Symbol	Description
%a	Day of week (abbreviated)
%A	Day of week
%b or %h	Month (abbreviated)
%B	Month
%c	Date and time in standard format
%C	Century
%d	Day of month (from 01 to 31)
%D	Date in abbreviated format (mm/dd/yy)
%e	Day of month as a 2-character string (from ' 1' to '31')
%g	Year according to the week number, 2 digits
%G	Year according to the week number, 4 digits
%H	Hour (from 00 to 23)
%I	Hour (from 01 to 12)

Symbol	Description
%j	Day of year (from 001 to 366)
%m	Month (from 01 to 12)
%M	Minute (from 00 to 59)
%n	Newline (\n)
%p	am or pm (or local equivalent)
%r	Time using a.m./p.m. notation
%R	Time using 24 hours notation
%S	Second (from 00 to 59)
%t	Tab (\t)
%T	Time in hh:ss:mm format
%u	Day of week (from 1 [Monday] to 7 [Sunday])
%U	Week number (Rule: The first Sunday is the first day of the first week.)
%V	Week number (Rule: The first week in the year with at least 4 days counts as week number 1.)
%w	Day of week (from 0 [Sunday] to 6 [Saturday])
%W	Week number (Rule: The first Monday is the first day of the first week.)
%x	Date in standard format (without the time)
%X	Time in standard format (without the date)
%y	Year (2 digits)
%Y	Year (4 digits)
%z or %Z	Time zone

Whenever it says *standard format* in Table 3.2, the formatting symbol gets replaced by the associated value according to the local setting. The preceding code changes the locale several times using setlocale() and

then calls strftime(). Note the differences shown in
Figure 3.1. Also take a look at Figure 3.2, in which the
same script was executed on a Windows machine.
According to the documentation, most of strftime()
also works on Windows, but on some configurations
changing the locale just does not seem to work.
Therefore, it is very important to test first whether the
system supports localized dates.

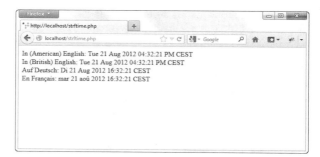

Figure 3.1   The current date in different locales

Figure 3.2   This particular system does not seem
to support locales

Manually Localizing Dates

```php
<?php
  $weekdays = array(
    'domingo', 'lunes', 'martes', 'miércoles',
    'jueves', 'viernes', 'sábado'
  );
  $months = array(
    'enero', 'febrero', 'marzo', 'abril',
    'mayo', 'junio', 'julio', 'agosto',
    'septiembre', 'octubre', 'noviembre', 'diciembre'
  );
  $weekday = date('w');
  $month = date('n');
  echo $weekdays[$weekday] . date(', j ') .
    $months[$month - 1] . date(' Y');
?>
```

If you cannot rely on setlocale(), yet want to use local-ized date and time values, you have to do the translations by yourself and store the results in an array. Then, you can use date() to retrieve information about a date. This serves as an index for your array.

The preceding code does this for both the day of the month and the month itself. One array contains the Spanish weekdays; another one contains the month names.

Note that the value for the month is decreased by one because the array $months has no dummy element at position 0; therefore, month number one (January) has the index 0.

Using the Current Date, the U.S./U.K./European Way

```php
<?php
  echo 'US format: ' . date('m/d/Y<b\r />');
  echo 'UK format: ' . date('d/m/Y<b\r />');
  echo 'German format: ' . date('d.m.Y<b\r />');
  echo 'International format: ' . date('Y-d-m');
?>
```

To give you a short and convenient reference, the preceding code contains several commonly used date formats. Depending on where you are, the order in which
day, month, and year are used might vary:

- In the United States, it's (mostly) month, day, and
  year.

- In the United Kingdom and the rest of Europe, it's
  (mostly) day, month, and year.

- The international standard date notation starts
  with the year and continues with month and day.

NOTE: The preceding code used a four-digit representation of the year because this is unambiguous. In practice, however, two-digit years are also commonly used.

Formatting a Specific Date

```php
<?php
  echo 'Time stamp: ' . mktime(12, 0, 0, 1, 1,
➥2001);
?>
```

All previous phrases in this chapter have used the current date and time. However, it is also possible to use
any other arbitrary date and time value. For this, the
relevant functions (especially `date()` and `strftime()`)
accept a second parameter—a time stamp of the date to
be analyzed. This time stamp is an integer value, the
date and time in the so-called epoch format. This is the
number of seconds that have passed since January 1,
1970, midnight Greenwich mean time (GMT)—the
beginning of the UNIX epoch. The time stamp/epoch
value of the current moment can be retrieved using
`time()` or by calling `date('U')` (see Table 3.1).

If you want to use another date, `mktime()` comes into
play. This function converts a date provided by year,
month, day, hour, minute, and second into an epoch
value. Probably the strangest thing about this function
is the order in which these parameters are passed:

1. Hour

2. Minute

3. Second

4. Month

5. Day

6. Year

You can also provide an optional seventh parameter,
regardless of whether it is daylight savings time (DST).
This is relevant close to the change from or to DST
because that does not happen at the same time over the
world.

The preceding code calculates the time stamp for noon
on the first day of this millennium. Because there was
no year 0, this was January 1, 2001.

NOTE: If you love collecting useless facts: On September 9, 2001, at precisely 3:46:40 a.m., the time stamp was 1,000,000,000. Therefore, `mktime(3, 46, 40, 9, 9, 2001)` returns 1000000000 (if your time zone is Central Europe).

Validating a Date

```php
<?php
  echo '2000 was ' .
    (checkdate(2, 29, 2000) ? 'a' : 'no') .
    ' leap year.<br />';
  echo '2100 will be ' .
    (checkdate(2, 29, 2100) ? 'a' : 'no') .
    ' leap year.';
?>
```

When you get a date—for example, from the user using an HTML form—this data must be validated. This includes checking whether the month exists and if the month has enough days. If it's February, you might also want to find out whether it is a leap year.

But PHP would not be PHP if you really had to do this on your own. The function `checkdate()` validates a date; you provide the month, the day, and the year as parameters.

TIP: Why was 2000 a leap year, but 2100 not? The definition says this: If a year is divisible by 4 and is either not divisible by 100 or is divisible by 400, it is a leap year and February has 29 days (this is because the Earth needs approximately 365.25 days to revolve around the sun). If you want to determine whether a given year is a leap year, this function comes in handy:

```
function isLeapYear($year) {
  return ($year % 4 == 0 &&
    ($year % 100 != 0 || $year % 400 == 0));
}
```

You could also use `DateTime::createFromFormat()`
which returns false if an error occurs. However
`checkdate()` is probably more explicit because the name
of the function describes exactly what we want to do.

Calculating a Relative Date

```
<?php
  echo 'The license you have just bought is valid
➥till ';
  $expiry = time() + 30 * 24 * 60 * 60; //30 days)
  echo strftime('%c', $expiry);
?>
```

Sometimes you have the task of calculating a date that
is relative to the current date (for example, 30 days
from now). Of course, you could put some real work
into actually calculating this value, taking into account
which day it is, whether it's a leap year, and whether
DST is relevant.

Far easier is the use of an epoch time stamp. Take, for
instance, the aforementioned task of finding a date that
lies 30 days in the future. One day has 24 hours, 1 hour
has 60 minutes, and 1 minute has 60 seconds.
Therefore, to get the current time stamp (using `time()`
or `date('U')`), you just need to add 30 + 24 + 60 +
60, and you have the time stamp of the desired date.
You can then use this time stamp to set a cookie's
expiry date or just to print out some information
about this date.

If you are using the DateTime class, you can also use the add() and sub() methods, which are covered in more detail in the "Calculating the Difference between Two Dates" section, later in this chapter.

Creating a Sortable Time Stamp

```php
<?php
  function timestamp($t = null) {
    if ($t == null) {
      $t = time();
    }
    return date('YmdHis', $t);
  }

  echo 'Time stamp: ' . timestamp(time());
?>
```

Using date values with a database is not always clever. Different language versions of the database, its drivers, or the underlying operating system could cause some trouble when the regional date formats do not fit together.

A potential alternative is the use of time stamps. Several different formats are available, but most of them have the following structure: year-month-day-hours-minutes-seconds. Using this value order, the string representation of the date can be easily sorted, which allows using it in databases.

To create such a time stamp, just a special call to date() is required. In the preceding code, this is encapsulated in a function for easy reuse.

TIP: This format is also used by MySQL for the representation of its TIMESTAMP data type.

Converting a String into a Date

```php
<?php
  echo 'Yesterday: ' . date('r',
➥strtotime('Yesterday')) . '<br />';
  echo 'Today: ' . date('r', strtotime('Today')) .
➥'<br />';
  echo 'Tomorrow: ' . date('r',
➥strtotime('Tomorrow')) . '<br />';
  echo 'In one week: ' . date('r', strtotime('+1
➥week')) . '<br />';
  echo 'One month before: ' . date('r', strtotime(
➥'-1 month')) . '<br />';
  echo 'Last Sunday: ' . date('r', strtotime('Last
➥Sunday')) . '<br />';
  echo 'Next fantasy day: ' .
    var_export(@date('r', strtotime('Next fantasy
➥day')), true);
?>
```

Previously, you saw a numeric representation of a date—either a triplet of day, month, and year, or a time stamp value. This time, you can go the other way and convert a string representation of a date/time value into an epoch value or something else that is usable within PHP and its date/time functions.

The whole magic is put into the PHP function strtotime(). According to the documentation, it "parse[s] about any English textual date/time description into a UNIX time stamp." It sounds amazing, and it is amazing. The basis for this is the GNU date syntax; the code at the beginning of this phrase shows some examples for strtotime().

NOTE: At the time of this writing, strtotime() shows some strange behavior when a relative date is calculated and a change from or to DST is imminent. Also at the time of this writing, PHP's date/time functions are about be rewritten and amended.

Determining Sunrise and Sunset

```php
<?php
  echo 'Sunrise: ' .
    date_sunrise(time(), SUNFUNCS_RET_STRING, 48,
➡11.5, 90, 1) . '<br />';
  echo 'Sunset: ' .
    date_sunset(time(), SUNFUNCS_RET_STRING, 48,
➡11.5, 90, 1);
?>
```

Depending on the current location and date, the times for sunrise and sunset can drastically vary. However, formulas exist for determining this value depending on latitude and longitude, and PHP has this functionality integrated into its core starting with PHP 5. All you are required to do is call date_sunrise() and date_sunset(). Both functions expect a number of parameters:

- A time stamp (epoch value) of the date for which to determine the sunrise/sunset.

- The desired format for the return value. SUFUNCS_RET_DOUBLE returns the time as a float value (between 0 and 23.99), SUNFUNCS_RET_STRING returns it as a string (between 00:00 and 23:59), and SUNFUNCS_RET_TIMESTAMP returns an epoch value.

- The latitude (northern latitude; use negative values for a southern latitude).

- The longitude (eastern longitude; use negative values for a western longitude).

- The zenith of the sunrise (in degrees).

- The offset (in hours) to GMT.

So, the preceding code calculates the sunrise and sunset for Munich, Germany, which resides at about 48° Northern latitude, 11° 30' eastern longitude, for the current day. I checked it: It worked!

Using Date and Time for Benchmarks

```php
<?php
 // ...

 $start = microtimestamp();
 $s = '';
 for ($i=0; $i < 100000; $i++) {
  $s .= "$i";
 }
 $end = microtimestamp();
 echo 'Using double quotes: ' . ($end-$start) .
➥'<br />';

 $start = microtimestamp();
 $s = '';
 for ($i=0; $i < 100000; $i++) {
  $s .= $i;
 }
 $end = microtimestamp();
 echo 'Using no quotes: ' . ($end-$start) . '<br
➥/>';
?>
```

Up to now, no date/time functions produced results that were more precise than to the second level; no microseconds were available. This changes when you use the function gettimeofday(), which returns an array of values. The key 'sec' returns the associated epoch value, and 'usec' returns the additional microseconds. With this, a very exact value can be used for operations that need exact measurement (for example, benchmarks).

The code at the beginning of this phrase contains a function microtimestamp() that returns an exact time stamp. This function is called twice; in between, a more-or-less complex calculation is done. The result of this is a benchmark that might help decide which coding technique is superior:

```
function microtimestamp() {
  $timeofday = gettimeofday();
  return $timeofday['sec'] + $timeofday['usec'] /
➥1000000;
}
```

Figure 3.3 shows the result. Your mileage might vary, but you will find that using the double quotes does not cost as much time as many people think—if any time at all.

Figure 3.3   Measuring the performance of two
pieces of code

TIP: You can replace the `microtimestamp()` function
with the following code:

```
function microtimestamp() {
  return microtime(true);
}
```

The function `microtime()` returns a float value of the
current microtime when the parameter `true` is provided
(this was added in PHP 5). However, this is reportedly
slower than using `gettimeofday()`, which just executes
the underlying `gettimeofday` system call.

Using Form Fields for Date Selection

```
<form method="post" action="action="">
➥<select name="day"><?php
    for ($i = 1; $i <= 31; $i++) {
      echo "<option value=\"$i\">$i</option>\n";
    }
```

```
  ?></select>
  <select name="month"><?php
    for ($i = 1; $i <= 12; $i++) {
      $monthname = date('F', mktime(12, 0, 0, $i, 1,
➥2012));
      echo "<option
➥value=\"$i\">$monthname</option>";
    }
  ?></select>
  <select name="year"><?php
    for ($i = 2012; $i <= 2015; $i++) {
      echo "<option value=\"$i\">$i</option>";
    }
  ?></select>
</form>
```

If you want to offer an HTML form to select a date, like many hotel- and flight-booking services offer, you can use the various parameters of date(); loop through all months of the year; and, thus, create a selection list of days, months, and years. The preceding code contains the syntax for this; see Figure 3.4 for the result.

Figure 3.4 The month names were automatically generated.

Create Self-Updating Form Fields for Date Selection

```php
<?php
  if (isset($_POST['month']) &&
➥is_numeric($_POST['month']) &&
    ((int)$_POST['month'] >= 1 &&
➥(int)$_POST['month'] <= 12)) {
    $month = (int)$_POST['month'];
  } else {
    $month = date('n');
  }
  if (isset($_POST['year']) &&
➥is_numeric($_POST['year']) &&
    ((int)$_POST['year'] >= 2012 &&
➥(int)$_POST['year'] <= 2015)) {
    $year = (int)$_POST['year'];
  } else {
  $year = date('Y');
  }
?>
<form method="post" action="<?php echo
➥htmlspecialchars($_SERVER['PHP_SELF']); ?>">
    $maxdays = date('t', mktime(12, 0, 0, $month, 1,
➥$year));
    for ($i = 1; $i <= $maxdays; $i++) {
      if (isset($_POST['day']) && $_POST['day'] ==
➥$i) {
        $sel = ' selected';
      } elseif ($i == date('j')) {
        $sel = ' selected';
      } else {
        $sel = '';
      }
      echo "<option value=\"$i\"$sel>$i</option>\n";
```

```
    }
  ?></select>
  // ...
</form>
```

The code from the preceding phrase has one minor flaw: The number of days per month is always from 1 to 31, even in months that have fewer days. Using JavaScript, it is possible to write a fancy script that calculates how many days the current month has and then updates the selection list.

However, it is much more convenient to use a combination of JavaScript and PHP. Using JavaScript, you automatically submit the form. Using PHP, you prefill the form fields (see Chapter 5, "Interacting with Web Forms," for more information about that) and, more important, find out how many days the related year has.

The JavaScript code is limited to a minimum: Selecting another month submits the HTML form (as does selecting another year because leap years make February longer):

```
<select name="month" onchange="this.form.submit();">
...
<select name="year" onchange="this.form.submit();">
```

The number of days per month can be found using date('t'). The listing at the beginning of this phrase contains the complete code for this, including some sanity checks for the information transmitted. In addition, the code automatically preselects the current date, unless the user chooses something else. Figure 3.5 contains the output of the complete code.

Figure 3.5 The PHP code filled the month selection list with the appropriate number of days.

Calculating the Difference between Two Dates

```php
<?php
  $century = mktime(12, 0, 0, 1, 1, 2001);
  $today = time();
  $difference = $today - $century;
  echo 'This century started ';
  echo floor($difference / 84600);
  $difference -= 84600 * floor($difference / 84600);
  echo ' days, ';
  echo floor($difference / 3600);
  $difference -= 3600 * floor($difference / 3600);
  echo ' hours, ';
  echo floor($difference / 60);
  $difference -= 60 * floor($difference / 60);
  echo " minutes, and $difference seconds ago.";
?>
```

The epoch value that can be determined by `time()` and other PHP functions can be used to easily calculate the difference between two dates. The trick is to convert the dates into time stamps (if not already available in this format). Then the difference between these two time stamps is calculated. The result is the time difference in seconds. This value can then be used to find out how many minutes, hours, and days this corresponds to:

- Divide the result by 60 to get the number of minutes.
- Divide the result by $60 \star 60 = 3,600$ to get the number of hours.
- Divide the result by $60 \star 60 \star 24 = 86,400$ to get the number of days.

If you start with the number of days, round down each result and subtract this from the result; you can also split up the difference into days, hours, and minutes.

A much more direct (and time zone / DST-aware) approach is provided by the `DateTime` class. It offers three methods that can help you calculate a date/time difference:

- `add()` adds an interval (`DateInterval` class) to a date.
- `sub()` subtracts an interval (`DateInterval` class) from a date.
- `diff()` calculates the difference between two `DateTime` instances, returning a `DateInterval` instance.

Creating a DateInterval instance can prove quite tricky. Some shortcuts exist, like for instance the following:

```
$i = DateInterval::createFromDateString('1 week');
```

For more specific intervals, however, take a look at the ISO 8601 duration specification. In short, it uses a format like this:

PnYnMnDTnHnMnS

Each lowercase n represents the number of units the following character stands for. For example, Y stands for the number of years, the first M for the number of months, and H for the number of hours; the T separates date information from time information. So, the following duration string means: one year, two months, and three hours:

P1Y2MT3H

Such a string can then be used in the DateInterval constructor:

```
$i = new DateInterval('P1Y2MT3H');
```

However, writing a DateInterval instance in a legible form is easier. Its format() method does all we need, using the control characters from Table 3.3.

Table 3.3   **Formatting Symbols for** DateInterval

Symbol	Description
%a	Total number of days
%d	Number of days, as a number
%D	Number of days, at least two digits
%h	Number of hours, as a number
%H	Number of hours, at least two digits

Table 3.3   Continued

Symbol	Description
%i	Number of minutes, as a number
%I	Number of minutes, at least two digits
%m	Number of months, as a number
%M	Number of months, at least two digits
%r	- when negative, empty string otherwise
%R	+ or -, depending on sign
%s	Number of seconds, as a number
%S	Number of seconds, at least two digits
%y	Number of years, as a number
%Y	Number of years, at least two digits
%%	Escaped percentage sign

Here is an example that would print +01:02:03:

```php
<?php
  $d1 = DateTime::createFromFormat('d.m.Y H:i:s',
'10.11.2012 23:34:45');
  $d2 = DateTime::createFromFormat('d.m.Y H:i:s',
'11.11.2012 00:36:48');
  $i = $d1->diff($d2);
  echo $i->format('%R%H:%I:%S');
?>
```

Using GMT Date/Time Information

Usually, PHP takes the local settings for time formats. However in some special cases, the GMT time format must be used. For this, PHP offers "GMT-enabled" versions of some of its date/time functions:

- gmdate() works like date() and formats a date/time value; however, the return value uses GMT format.

- gmmktime() creates a time stamp like mktime(); however, it uses GMT.

- gmstrftime() formats a time as strftime() does; however, it uses GMT.

GMT is important when it comes to setting a page's expiry date in an HTTP header or manually setting the expiry date of a cookie, also in the HTTP header.

What Does PEAR Offer?

The following PHP Extension and Application Repository (PEAR) packages offer functionality helpful for processing form data of any kind:

- Date contains a set of functions to work with various date/time values, including conversions between time zones and various date/time representations.

- Date_Holidays calculates the names and dates of special holidays.

4

Working with Objects (and Related Topics)

Object-oriented programming (OOP) is one of the most commonly used programming paradigms today. PHP was not conceived as an object-oriented language in the beginning, but it added some limited OOP support in PHP 4 and a lot more in PHP 5.x.

Because this is a phrasebook, OOP is not as well-suited as most of the other topics in this book. OOP phrases tend to be very long, or very specific to a given scenario, or so general that they might be considered common knowledge (without the need to look them up very often).

We considered several ideas, but ultimately we decided to present a mix of various OOP and OOP-related topics, phrases that show useful but nontrivial OOP features of PHP, phrases that explain fundamental constructs, and more. When using OOP, most of the time it is experience that matters, but this chapter will still provide a lot of information you will want to refer to from time to time.

Setting Up Classes

```
class MyClass {
}
```

This phrase gives you a concise (and certainly incomplete) rundown of the most important OOP basics from a PHP point of view. The central element of the concept of OOP is a class. A class may contain constants, properties, and methods. Visibility keywords public, protected, and private denote who may access which property or method.

If a class is instantiated (with new), the $this keyword provides a reference to the calling object. If the class contains a method called __construct(), this method will be called upon instantiation of the class:

```php
<?php
  class MyClass {
    private $prop = null;

    public function setProperty($value) {
      $this->prop = $value;
    }

    public function getProperty() {
      return $this->prop;
    }

    public function __construct($value = null) {
      if ($value !== null) {
        $this->prop = $value;
      }
    }
  }
```

```php
  $c = new MyClass('abc');
  echo $c->getProperty();
?>
```

Implementing a Class (class.php)

NOTE: The three available visibility levels are as follows:

- **public**—Accessible from everywhere
- **protected**—Accessible only from within the class, and from derived classes, and from instances of the same class or derived class
- **private**—Accessible only from within the class, and from instances of the same class

---

It is also possible to access class properties or methods without having an instance by using a *static* context (and the static keyword). It is obvious that static methods do not have access to $this. However, self provides the current class:

```php
<?php
  class MyStaticClass {
    private static $prop = 'abc';

    public static function getProperty() {
      return self::$prop;
    }
  }

  echo MyStaticClass::getProperty();
?>
```

Implementing a Class with a Static Method and Property (static.php)

Understanding Inheritance

```
class MyDerivedClass extends MyBaseClass {
}
```

A class can be inherited from another class by using the extends keyword. As a consequence, the new class contains (inherits) all public and protected methods from the base class. Of course, it is possible to overwrite these methods in the derived classes.

Access to the parent class is granted by the parent keyword. The associated syntax looks like a static reference, but isn't one—so you can use $this within the called method.

The code in Listing 4.3 overwrites the constructor in the derived class, but also calls the parent constructor. Note that the signatures of the two constructors are different. The main code also calls a method from the base class:

```php
<?php
  class MyBaseClass {
    protected $value1 = null;
    protected $value2 = null;

    protected function __construct($value = null) {
      if ($value !== null) {
        $this->value1 = $value;
      }
    }

    public function getValue1() {
      return $this->value1;
    }
```

```
  }

  class MyDerivedClass extends MyBaseClass {
    protected $value2 = null;

    public function __construct($value1 = null,
➥$value2 = null) {
      if ($value1 !== null) {
        parent::__construct($value1);
        if ($value2 !== null) {
          $this->value2 = $value2;
        }
      }
    }

    public function getValue2() {
      return $this->value2;
    }
  }

  $c = new MyDerivedClass('abc', 'def');
  echo '1: ', $c->getValue1(), ', 2:', $c-
➥>getValue2();
?>
```

Using Inheritance with PHP (extends.php)

NOTE: PHP does not support multiple inheritance, so
one class may be derived only from (exactly) one other
class. Of course, you could derive class B from class A,
and class C from class B, so that class C also inherits
public and protected methods from A.

Using Abstract Classes and Interfaces

```
abstract class MyAbstractBaseClass {
}
```

PHP supports two additional ways of inheritance: abstract classes and interfaces. The two approaches are similar, but the differences are essential. The common goal is to provide a contract or blueprint for a derived class: the base class (or classes, as discussed later) defines which methods are expected in the new class.

When you use an abstract class, the inheritance is done as before, using the `extends` keyword. However, what's new is that the base class is defined as abstract, thanks to the `abstract` keyword. Also, a set of methods within the abstract class can be labeled as abstract, as well, but these do not contain any code:

```
protected abstract function myMethod();
```

The derived class now absolutely needs to implement those methods, using the same signatures, and also the same (or at least a less restrictive) visibility setting. For instance, if the abstract base class defines an abstract protected method, the derived class needs to implement this method as protected or as public. If you are using type hints, these need to be identical, as well.

If the abstract method contains additional methods that are not declared as abstract, they are inherited as with regular classes, too, as long as they are protected or public:

```php
<?php
  abstract class MyAbstractBaseClass {
    protected $value1 = null;
    protected $value2 = null;

    protected function getValue1() {
      return $this->value1;
    }

    protected function getValue2() {
      return $this->value2;
    }

    protected abstract function dumpData();
  }

  class MyAbstractClass extends MyAbstractBaseClass
➥{
    public function __construct($value1 = null,
➥$value2 = null) {
      if ($value1 !== null) {
        $this->value1 = $value1;
        if ($value2 !== null) {
          $this->value2 = $value2;
        }
      }
    }

    public function dumpData() {
      echo '1: ', $this->getValue1(), ', 2:',
➥$this->getValue2();
    }
  }

  $c = new MyAbstractClass('ghi', 'jkl');
  $c->dumpData();
?>
```

Using an Abstract Class (abstract.php)

As with regular classes, abstract classes support single inheritance only.

The "same same but different" approach uses interfaces. An interface looks like a regular PHP class, but uses the `interface` keyword rather than `class`. The interface does not contain any implementation at all, just function signatures. All of these functions need to be public.

The actual class now "inherits" from this interface; in this context, however, we say that the class *implements* the interface. This is emphasized by the `implements` keyword, which is used rather than `extends`.

The other rules are very similar to those of abstract classes: All methods from the interface need to be implemented, and the function signatures need to stay the same (including the visibility level, which is public anyway). As an additional benefit, a class may implement multiple interfaces simultaneously, as long as all interfaces involved have distinct method names.

The following code creates two interfaces and then implements both of them in one class:

```php
<?php
  interface MyInterface1 {
    public function getValue1();
    public function getValue2();
  }

  interface MyInterface2 {
    public function dumpData();
  }

  class MyInterfaceClass implements MyInterface1,
➥MyInterface2 {
```

```
   protected $value1 = null;
   protected $value2 = null;

   public function __construct($value1 = null,
➡$value2 = null) {
     if ($value1 !== null) {
       $this->value1 = $value1;
       if ($value2 !== null) {
         $this->value2 = $value2;
       }
     }
   }

   public function getValue1() {
     return $this->value1;
   }

   public function getValue2() {
     return $this->value2;
   }

   public function dumpData() {
     echo '1: ', $this->getValue1(), ', 2:',
➡$this->getValue2();
   }
 }

 $c = new MyInterfaceClass('mno', 'pqr');
 $c->dumpData();
?>
```

Using an Interface (interface.php)

Preventing Inheritance and Overwriting

```
final class MyFinalBaseClass {}
public final function myMethod() {}
```

There are some classes you do not want to inherit from (for instance, if they contain critical functionality, and you do not want the other developers overwrite those vital methods). PHP's final keyword is suited for that task. You can either make a class final (in which case, it is not possible to inherit from it at all) or you can declare a method as final (in which case, code cannot overwrite it). Therefore, the following code causes an exception, as depicted in Figure 4.1:

```php
<?php
  class MyFinalBaseClass {
    public final function getCopyrightNotice() {
      return '&copy; by Original Author';
    }
  }

  class MyFinalClass extends MyFinalBaseClass {
    function getCopyrightNotice() {
      return '&copy; by me!';
    }
  }
?>
```

Preventing Overloading with the final Keyword (final.php)

Figure 4.1   Final methods cannot be overwritten.

Of course, if you are the sole developer making a class or method final does not seem to be necessary. However, you should always be ready for when the development team gets larger or you refactor your codebase into a library others will also be using.

Using Autoloading

```
spl_autoload_register('myAutoloadFunction');
```

When you are using a class, it needs to be defined; otherwise PHP will throw an error. There is a second chance, however, should a class not be available once it is used. The `spl_autoload_register()` function registers a function that will be called once PHP code tries to use a class that has not been registered yet. After the call to the registration function, the code that uses the undefined class is run again. If the class is now available, great; otherwise, the usual error occurs.

A common pattern is to use a fixed naming scheme for files containing classes and to put the classes in a defined directory. For instance, the class MyClass resides in the file /classes/MyClass.class.php. In that case, the following autoloading function would load the class on demand:

```php
<?php
  function myAutoloadFunction($classname) {
    if (preg_match('/^[a-zA-Z_\x7f-\xff][a-zA-Z0-
➥9_\x7f-\xff]*$/', $classname)) {
      //check for valid classname
      require_once
➥"/path/to/classes/$classname.class.php";
    }
  }

  spl_autoload_register('myAutoloadFunction');
?>
```

Autoloading Classes (autoload.php)

So, for instance, the following call

```php
$c = new UnknownClass();
```

would in turn call myAutoloadFunction(), providing UnknownClass as the value for the $classname parameter.

If you call spl_autoload_register() multiple times, all autoloading functions are registered, so PHP calls each of them until the desired class is finally defined—or until all such functions have been called.

NOTE: The spl_autoload_register() function was introduced in PHP 5.1.2 as part of the SPL (Standard PHP Library). Formerly, you had to write a function

called __autoload() and put your autoloading code
there. At some point in the future, __autoload() might
be removed to PHP, so it is more forward compatible to
use spl_autoload_register() instead.

NOTE: PHP also provides functionality for accessing
class methods and class properties that do not exist:

- If a class method is called but does not exist, the
  class's __call() method is executed, if it exists.
- If a class property is accessed but does not
  exist, the class's __get() and __set() methods
  are executed (for read and write access), if they
  exist.

Cloning Objects

```
$b = clone $a;
```

Suppose you have a class instance in $a. The assign-
ment $b = $a would not create a copy of $a, but $b
would now contain a reference to $a; you would still
have only one class instance.

As an alternative, PHP provides the clone keyword,
which allows creating a copy of the class:

```
$b = clone $a;
```

However, sometimes you do not want *exact* copies. For
instance, imagine that each class instance has a property
that contains a globally unique identifier (GUID).
Even though you create a clone of a class instance, you
want the GUID still to be as unique as possible.

PHP provides a way to inject code after an object has
been cloned. If the class contains a method called
__clone(), it is executed for the cloned class instance
after the cloning process has finished:

```php
<?php
  class MyCloneableClass {
    private $guid = null;

    public function __construct() {
      $this->guid = uniqid();
    }

    public function __clone() {
      $this->guid = uniqid();
    }

    public function getGuid() {
      return $this->guid;
    }
  }

  $c1 = new MyCloneableClass();
  $c2 = clone $c1;
  echo '1: ', $c1->getGuid(), ', 2:', $c2-
➥>getGuid();
?>
```

Cloning Objects (and Changing Them Nevertheless) (clone.php)

Running the preceding code leads to a result comparable to Figure 4.2: The two instances have different
GUIDs.

Figure 4.2   The two instances have different GUIDs.

Serializing and Deserializing Objects

```php
public function __sleep() {
  $this->db->close();
  return array('guid');
}
public function __wakeup() {
  $this->connectDb();
}
```

When you are storing objects for later use, they need to be transformed into something that can easily be put in, say, a database. PHP provides several ways to transform an object instance into a string (and putting it back into its original form); the most common approach is to use the serialize() and deserialize() functions, which are also used in other chapters of this book.

Interesting from an OOP point of view is that it is possible to intercept the process of serialization and deserialization. Suppose, for instance, that your class contains a property that should (or can) not be serialized (perhaps a database handle). Ideally, this property should be removed before serialization and re-created upon deserialization.

PHP aids us with this task and provides the following two "magic" method names. If your class contains these methods, they will be executed accordingly:

- __sleep()—Needs to return an array with all properties to be serialized, may also clean up

- __wakeup()—Is called after deserialization, can be used to re-setup properties

The following code listing shows a typical implementation closing and resetting a database connection. After serialization and deserialization, the GUID is the same, but the database connection has been reestablished:

```php
<?php
  class MySerializableClass {
    public $guid = null;
    public $db = null;

    public function __construct() {
      $this->guid = uniqid();
      $this->connectDb();
    }

    private function connectDb() {
      $this->db = new MySQLi('server', 'user',
➥'password', 'db');
    }

    public function __sleep() {
      $this->db->close();
      return array('guid');
```

```php
  }

  public function __wakeup() {
    $this->connectDb();
  }
}

$c1 = new MySerializableClass();
echo 'Before: ', $c1->guid;
$s = serialize($c1);
$c2 = unserialize($s);
echo '; after: ', $c2->guid;
?>
```

Serializing and Deserializing Objects (serialize.php)

NOTE: When deserializing an object, you need to make sure that the class exists; otherwise, PHP uses the dreaded "special" __PHP_Incomplete_Class_Name class in the result.

TIP: PHP supports a variety of magic methods and functions. The online manual features a list at http://php.net/oop5.magic.

Implementing Singletons

```php
if (self::$instance == null) {
  self::$instance = new self;
}
return self::$instance;
```

A common—but also criticized—design pattern is the singleton pattern. It is not entirely easy to implement, so we have dedicated a phrase to its creation.

The main goal of using the singleton pattern is that no matter how often you instantiate a certain class, you only get one object. This can, for instance, prove useful when creating database connections: often, you only need one connection that can be reused within your code.

A common PHP implementation of the singleton pattern uses a few OOP features of the language to prevent multiple different instances of one class. First of all, the class constructor is not available because we make it private:

```
private function __construct() {
}
```

Another approach to create two instance of the class is to use one instance and then clone it. This can be avoided by making the __clone() magic method private, as well:

```
private function __clone() {
}
```

So, right now we cannot create multiple instances of the class; we cannot even create *one* instance. Therefore, we introduce a method that will give us a class instance. Within the class, we can call the class constructor—the private visibility allows that. The class instance will then be stored in a static and private class member. So, the dummy instantiation method first checks whether we already have a class instance stored in that static property. If so, the instance is returned; otherwise, the code creates a new (and only) instance:

```
static private $instance = null;

static public function getInstance() {
  if (self::$instance == null) {
    self::$instance = new self;
  }
  return self::$instance;
}
```

The following code listing contains the complete syntax for the singleton class:

```php
<?php
  class PHPSingleton{
    static private $instance = null;

    static public function getInstance() {
      if (self::$instance == null) {
        self::$instance = new self;
      }
      return self::$instance;
    }

    private function __construct() {
    }
    private function __clone() {
    }
  }
?>
```

Implementing a Singleton (singleton.php)

NOTE: As mentioned, singleton patterns have some shortcomings. Code generally gets harder to test because the singleton class needs to be global and adds state to the application. As always, your mileage may vary.

Using Namespaces

One major new feature of PHP 5.3 is the inclusion of namespaces. Namespaces are a tool to group related functionality and to avoid name clashes. Imagine you write a function with the generic name such as showInfo(). Another developer in the same project writes a different function but uses the same name. Usually, you would prefix the function name so that it is unique, which leads to the dreaded, really long identifiers, like Project_Module_Submodule_showInfo(). Namespaces can help here: You provide the context in form of a namespace; within that namespace, showInfo() is unique; the other developers use other namespaces. In the end, this facilitates encapsulation of functionality.

The main keyword for namespaces is—surprise!— namespace. The namespace keyword must be the first command within a PHP page (after optional comments) and must even not be preceded by HTML markup. If you would like to structure namespaces, you may create a hierarchy, by using the (a bit unusual) backslash character as a separator:

```
namespace Project\Module\Submodule;
```

This namespace is now valid for the whole file. If you create the showInfo() method within that file, and include the file in another PHP script, the following code can be used to execute the method:

```
Project\Module\Submodule\showInfo();
```

To define several namespaces in one file, you could use multiple namespace statements; the preferred way however is to use curly braces:

```
namespace Namespace1 {
  // ...
}

namespace Namespace2 {
  // ...
}
```

For using namespaces, PHP offers several options. Of course, you can provide the fully qualified namespace name, as in the previous example; a relative syntax is supported, too. A more convenient way for local namespaces is to use an alias. The syntax use <namespace> or use <namespace> as <alias> can significantly save typing and facilitate namespace access. Here is one example where a namespace only is imported:

```
import Project\Module\Submodule;
Submodule\showInfo();
```

When you are using an alias, the code could look like this:

```
import Project\Module\Submodule as Mod;
Mod\showInfo();
```

Within a namespace, accessing built-in PHP classes seems to be a challenge at first because PHP looks for those classes within the current namespace. But prefixing the class name with a backslash does the trick, and lets PHP look in the global class list:

```
namespace Project\Module\Submodule;
$c = new \SoapClient('file.wsdl');
```

There is so much more to discuss regarding namespaces, but to be true to the phrasebook concept, we just focus on how namespaces work (in a nutshell). The PHP online manual contains much more information at http://php.net/namespace.

Using Traits

```
class MyTraitClass {
  use MyTrait1, MyTrait2 {
    MyTrait1::showTime as now;
    MyTrait2::showCopyright insteadof MyTrait1;
  }
}
```

One of the new features in PHP 5.4 is support for traits, a means for code reuse. A trait is a collection of functions, a kind of class without instantiation. In order to use this new feature, you must create a trait by using the trait keyword.

```
trait MyTrait1 {
  public function showTime() {
    $date = new DateTime('now');
    echo $date->format('H:i:s');
  }
}
```

Then, within a class, you can load the traits, with the use keyword. The methods are then at your disposal:

```
class MyTraitClass {
  use MyTrait1;
}

$c = new MyTraitClass();
$c->showTime();
```

You can also use several traits within one class. In that case, however, you need to be careful if several traits define the same methods. Then you would get an error message, just like with interfaces with the same method names. Unlike with interfaces, however, traits offer a way to prevent this error. When loading the trait, you

can resolve these naming conflicts with the instanceof
operator. Suppose, for example, that there are two traits,
MyTrait1 and MyTrait2, both defining the showTime()
method. The following syntax would make sure that no
error occurs and that the showTime() implementation
from MyTrait1 is used and not the one from MyTrait2:

```php
class MyTraitClass {
  use MyTrait1, MyTrait2{
    MyTrait1::showTime insteadof MyTrait2;
  }
}
```

Another feature is the use of an alias, using the as
keyword, or even the use of abstract methods within
the trait. The following code listing uses two traits,
insteadof, and an alias, and returns an output similar
to the one in Figure 4.3:

```php
<?php
  trait MyTrait1 {
    public function showTime() {
      $date = new DateTime('now');
      echo $date->format('H:i:s');
    }

    public function showCopyright() {
      echo '&copy; Trait 1';
    }
  }

  trait MyTrait2 {
    public function showCopyright() {
      echo '&copy; Trait 2';
    }
  }
```

```
class MyTraitClass {
  use MyTrait1, MyTrait2 {
    MyTrait1::showTime as now;
    MyTrait2::showCopyright insteadof MyTrait1;
  }
}

$c = new MyTraitClass();
$c->now();
echo '<hr />';
$c->showCopyright();
?>
```

Using Two Traits (trait.php)

Figure 4.3   The copyright method from the second trait is used.

5

Interacting with Web Forms

HTML forms are one of the key ingredients of any dynamic Web site because they can enable the users of a site to interact with it. Otherwise, Web sites are more or less static: They may be driven by a database and, therefore, regularly changing, but they look the same for each and every visitor. HTML forms can change that; therefore, using data from forms within PHP is very important.

Reading the information in is a very easy task: For form data submitted via GET (that is, in the uniform resource identifier [URI] of the page requested), the data can be found in $_GET[<value of name attribute of form field>]. $_GET[<value of name attribute of form field>] holds the field data if the form has been submitted via POST. However, this is only the beginning. Suppose a user fills out a form but forgets one field. Instead of an error message asking the user to click the browser's Back button, the user can expect a form in which all fields are filled in with the values that he previously provided. Many books neglect this; yet, even worse, some books just do it wrong. You must not forget the special encoding of the form field values; otherwise, the form is subject to Cross-Site Scripting (XSS) attacks or, at least, could look ugly. Figure 5.1 demonstrates this: You see two buttons with the same caption; however, only the first button's caption was encoded correctly in the HTML code.

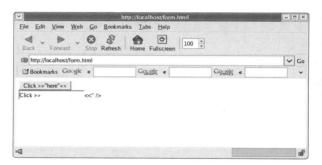

Figure 5.1   Correct encoding of special characters is mandatory.

Other important topics of interest include Hypertext Transfer Protocol (HTTP) file uploads and coping with the various settings in php.ini or elsewhere that might boycott the good intentions of the developer.

Sending Form Data Back to the Current Script

```
<form action="<?php echo
➥htmlspecialchars($_SERVER['PHP_SELF']); ?>">
</form>
```

All relevant browsers send back form data to the current page, if no action attribute is provided in the <form> element. However, the HTML and the Extensible

Hypertext Markup Language (XHTML) specifications both state that `action` is a required attribute (marked as `#REQUIRED` in the Document Type Definitions [DTDs]). The behavior of the user agent is undefined, as the HTML specification at http://w3.org/TR/html4/ interact/forms.html#adef-action explains. Therefore, it's a good idea to specifically provide the uniform resource locator (URL) of the current script as the form's action. The code above does this and also escapes special characters in `$_SERVER['PHP_SELF']` for security reasons. An even easier (and still effective) way is to set the `action` attribute to an empty string (`""`).

Reading Out Form Data

In very early versions of PHP, reading out form data was very easy: If the form field had the `name` attribute `"whatever"` or, in newer versions of HTML/XHTML, the `id` attribute `"whatever"`, PHP created a variable `$whatever` in the global scope. This was very convenient, but, from an architectural point of view, was and is a bad idea. Therefore, this was disabled by default from PHP version 4.2 onward using the following `php.ini` directive:

```
register_globals = Off
```

Since PHP 3, the following global arrays have been available for form data:

- `$HTTP_GET_VARS`—All data provided using `GET`
- `$HTTP_POST_VARS`—All data provided using `POST`
- `$HTTP_REQUEST_VARS`—All data provided using `GET` or `POST`, or via cookies (use not recommended)

These arrays are global; therefore, you have to use the

global keyword to uplevel them to global scope if you use them within a function:

```
function processData() {
  global $HTTP_POST_VARS;
  // now you may access $HTTP_POST_VARS
}
```

However, these arrays can be deactivated (PHP 5 onward), as well, using this php.ini directive:

```
register_long_arrays = Off
```

Therefore, the following is the only recommended method to access form data today in PHP:

- $_GET for GET data
- $_POST for POST data
- $_FILES for file uploads via POST
- $_REQUEST for POST, GET, and cookies (not recommended)

The keys of these arrays are the names of the form values. The $_* arrays are so-called superglobal arrays—that is, you do not have to use the global keyword to get them into global scope; they are already available within functions.

After deciding which superglobal array to use (depending on the form's method), accessing form data is easy: $_GET[<formfieldname>] or $_POST[<formfieldname>] retrieves the value in the form element. Table 5.1 shows which data is returned for which form field type.

Table 5.1   **Form Field Types and Data Returned in
$GET/$POST**

Form Field Type	Data Returned
Text field	Text in field
Password field	Text in field (clear text, not encrypted)
Multiline text field	Text in field
Hidden field	value attribute of field
Radio button	value attribute of selected radio button
Check box	value attribute of check box if checked (or usually "on", if value not set)
Selection list	value attribute of selected list element (or caption of selected list element, if value not set)
Multiple selection list	value attributes of selected list elements as an array (or captions of selected list elements as an array, if values not set)
Submit button	value attribute of Submit button, if this one was used to send the form (important if there is more than one Submit button)

TIP: Two remaining form field types, graphical Submit buttons and file uploads, are covered specifically later in this chapter.

Checking Whether a Form Has Been Submitted

```php
<?php
  if (isset($_POST['Submit'])) {
    echo '<h1>Thank you for filling out this
➥form!</h1>';
  } else {
?>
  <form method="post" action="<?php echo
➥htmlspecialchars($_SERVER['PHP_SELF']); ?>">
    <input type="submit" name="Submit" value="Submit
➥form" />
  </form>
<?php
  }
?>
```

When both the HTML form and the processing PHP code are on the same page (something that is recommended when it comes to prefilling forms), it is important to find out whether a form is just called in the browser (using GET) or if the form is submitted (and the data must be processed).

You can take several different approaches to this task; something that always works is assigning the Submit button a name and then testing whether this name is present when the form is submitted.

TIP: If your form has multiple Submit buttons, give each of them a distinctive name; then, you can check specifically for this name and, therefore, determine which Submit button has been used.

Saving Form Data into a Cookie

```php
function setCookieData($arr) {
  $formdata = getCookieData();
  if ($formdata == null) {
    $formdata = array();
  }
  foreach ($arr as $name => $value) {
    $formdata[$name] = $value;
  }
  setcookie('formdata', serialize($formdata),
➥time()+30*24*60*60);
}
```

After the form has been submitted, the data must go
somewhere, possibly in a database (see Chapters 8,
"Working with MySQL Databases," and 9, "Working
with Other Databases"), in a file, or sent via email.
When a Web site contains several similar forms (for
example, forms that all require the user to provide his
name and contact information), it is a good idea to save
the data after the user fills it in. Because HTTP is a
stateless protocol, you have to use cookies (see Chapter
7, "Using Files on the Server File System")—sessions
are useless because they expire when the user closes the
browser.

Because user agents only have to save 20 cookies per
domain (although they might store more), it's a good
idea to store the form information in one cookie, in
the form of an array. However, only string values are
allowed in cookies; this is why you have to serialize the
array. Also be aware that you usually can only store a
bit less than 4KB of data in a cookie; the rest may get
truncated.

The function shown in the listing at the beginning of this phrase writes the contents of the array provided as a parameter into the cookie.

The function getCookieData() returns the existing data from the cookie (if available) and unserializes it into an array. You will see the code in a later phrase.

The only thing left to do is to write the required form data into this array. You can specifically submit only certain values, or the complete array $_GET or $_POST, as shown in the following code:

```php
<?php
  require_once 'getFormData.inc.php';
  if (isset($_POST['Submit'])) {
    setCookieData($_POST);
  }
?>
...
<?php
  if (isset($_POST['Submit'])) {
    echo '<h1>Thank you for filling out this
➥form!</h1>';
  } else {
?>
  <form method="post" action="<?php echo
➥htmlspecialchars($_SERVER['PHP_SELF']); ?>">
  ...
  </form>
<?php
  }
?>
```

Figure 5.2 shows the resulting cookie.

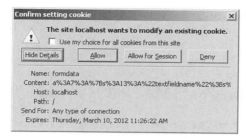

Figure 5.2   The serialized form data is saved in a cookie.

NOTE: Note that you have to save the form data prior to any HTML output. Because cookies are sent as part of the HTTP header, they have to be declared before HTML starts (and, as a matter of consequence, the HTTP header ends). You can find more information about the timing of cookies in Chapter 6.

Prefilling Text Fields and Password Fields

```
<input type="text" name="textfieldname"
  value="<?php
  echo (isset($_POST['textfieldname'])) ?
➥htmlspecialchars($_POST['textfieldname']) : '';
  ?>" />
```

The value in a text field (and in a password field and in a hidden field, as well) is provided in its value attribute. However, the data there must be properly encoded with htmlspecialchars() to get rid of dangerous characters such as " or < or >. The code snippet in the preceding code expects the form to be submitted back to itself; thus, it extracts the current value of the text field from $_POST (it would work analogously with $_GET). This works for password fields and hidden fields, as well (although it is considered bad practice to prefill password fields, since the "secret" data in there is not encrypted in HTML).

NOTE: If you also want to escape the single quote (') character, use `htmlspecialchars()` in the following fashion:

```
htmlspecialchars($_POST['textfieldname'],
➥ENT_QUOTES)
```

Because in our form all HTML attributes are delimited by double quotes, we do not need to specifically escape single quotes. If you are using single quotes, however, you absolutely need to escape then within attribute values.

If you want to use a default value for this form element, you just have to provide this default value rather than the empty string in the PHP code:

```
<input type="text" name="textfieldname"
  value="<?php
➥echo (isset($_POST['textfieldname'])) ?
htmlspecialchars($_POST['textfieldname']) : 'default
➥value';
  ?>" />
```

Another possibility is to prefill form values from cookies. This is quite useful when users enter their data into a form several times. So, when they visit a form on the site a couple of days later, the old data can be retrieved from the cookie. Yes, just 1 cookie because only 20 cookies per domain are allowed. We use an array for that, of course. However, only strings are allowed as cookie values, so the use of serialize() and unserialize() is required.

The following function retrieves a value from the cookie that contains the form data. The order of precedence is by default (but can be changed by the variables_order php.ini setting) as follows: If $_GET or $_POST contains a current value for this field, this value is used. (Specific versions of the function exist for $_GET and $_POST because only one of these two methods is normally used at a time.) Otherwise, the script looks in $_COOKIE for an associated value. If nothing is found, an empty string is returned:

```php
function getCookieData() {
  if (isset($_COOKIE['formdata'])) {
    $formdata = $_COOKIE['formdata'];
    if ($formdata != '') {
      if (get_magic_quotes_gpc()) {
        $formdata = stripslashes($formdata);
      }
      return unserialize($formdata);
    } else {
      return array();
    }
  } else {
    return null;
  }
}

function getFormDataPOST($name) {
  if (isset($_POST[$name])) {
    return $_POST[$name];
  } else {
    $cookiedata = getCookieData();
    if ($cookiedata != null &&
      isset($cookiedata[$name])) {
```

```
      return $cookiedata[$name];
    }
  }
  return '';
}
function getFormDataGET($name) {
  if (isset($_GET[$name])) {
    return $_GET[$name];
  } else {
    $cookiedata = getCookieData();
    if ($cookiedata != null &&
      isset($cookiedata[$name])) {
      return $cookiedata[$name];
    }
  }
  return '';
}
```

Now, prefilling the form value is easy: Because
getFormDataGET() and getFormDataPOST() always return
anything—including an empty string—the return value
can be directly used in the text field's value attribute:

```
<?php
  require_once 'getFormData.inc.php';
?>
...
<input type="text" name="textfieldname"
  value="<?php
    echo
➥htmlspecialchars(getFormDataPOST('textfieldname'));
  ?>" />
```

Prefilling Multiline Text Fields

```
<textarea cols="40" rows="5"
➥name="areafieldname"><?php
  echo (isset($_POST['areafieldname'])) ?
➥htmlspecialchars($_POST['areafieldname']) : '';
  ?></textarea>
```

With multiline text fields, almost the same approach as
with single-line text fields and password fields can be
used. The only difference is the location where to put
the prefill value: It belongs between <textarea> and
</textarea>, as shown in the preceding code.

NOTE: If you want to provide a default value in the multiline text field (for example, "Enter your data here"),
provide this instead of the empty string in the PHP
code. Remember that line feeds are possible, as well:

```
<?php
  echo (isset($_POST['areafieldname'])) ?
➥htmlspecialchars($_POST['areafieldname']) :
"default\nvalue";
?>
```

Using the combined cookie/GET or cookie/POST
approach, the code simplifies a bit:

```
<?php
  require_once 'getFormData.inc.php';
?>
...
<textarea cols="40" rows="5" name="
➥areafieldname"><?php
  echo htmlspecialchars(getFormDataPOST
➥('areafieldname'));
  ?></textarea>
```

Preselecting Radio Buttons

```
<input type="radio" name="groupname" value="php52"
➡<?php
  if (isset($_POST['groupname']) && $_POST
➡['groupname'] == 'php52') {
    echo 'checked="checked" ';
  }
?>/>PHP 5.2
<input type="radio" name="groupname" value="php53"
➡<?php
  if (isset($_POST['groupname']) && $_POST
➡['groupname'] == 'php53') {
    echo 'checked="checked" ';
  }
?>/>PHP 5.3
<input type="radio" name="groupname" value="php54"
➡<?php
  if (isset($_POST['groupname']) && $_POST
➡['groupname'] == 'php54') {
    echo 'checked="checked" ';
  }
?>/>PHP 5.4
```

A group of radio buttons is identified by the common
name attribute. Out of a group of buttons, only one can
be selected (or none). When submitting a form to the
server, the value attribute of the selected radio buttons
is transmitted to the server. Therefore, it is quite messy
but rather trivial to prefill a group of radio buttons: Just
compare the value in $_GET/$_POST with the associated
value. If it fits, print out checked, the HTML attribute
that preselects a radio button, as shown in the preceding code.

This code can be extended so that a radio button is
preselected when the user has previously saved his

selection in a cookie, using the include file
getFormData.inc.php, as shown in the following code:

```php
<?php
  require_once 'getFormData.inc.php';
?>
...
<input type="radio" name="groupname" value="php52"
➥<?php
  if (getFormDataPOST('groupname') == 'php52') {
    echo 'checked="checked" ';
  }
?>/>PHP 5.2
<input type="radio" name="groupname" value="php53"
➥<?php
  if (getFormDataPOST('groupname') == 'php53') {
    echo 'checked="checked" ';
  }
?>/>PHP 53
<input type="radio" name="groupname" value="php54"
➥<?php
  if (getFormDataPOST('groupname') == 'php54') {
    echo 'checked="checked" ';
  }
?>/>PHP 5.4
```

Preselecting Check Boxes

```php
<input type="checkbox" name="boxname" value="yes"
➥<?php
  if (isset($_POST['boxname']) && $_POST['boxname']
➥== 'yes') {
    echo 'checked="checked" ';
  }
?>/>I agree.
```

Although some Web sites pretend to group check boxes
like radio buttons, this is technically not true. Every
check box stands on its own; therefore, they all should
have different names; it would not make sense to give
them identical names. Then each check box can be
treated individually: Check for the associated value
attribute, and then print out the checked HTML attribute you find a match.

When using cookie data (if available), the code changes
slightly:

```php
<?php
  require_once 'getFormData.inc.php';
?>
...
<input type="checkbox" name="boxname" value="yes"
➥<?php
  if (getFormDataPOST('boxname') == 'yes') {
    echo 'checked="checked" ';
  }
?>/>I agree.
```

Preselecting Selection Lists

```php
<select name="listname">
  <option value="php52"<?php
  if (isset($_POST['listname']) && $_POST
➥['listname'] == 'php52') {
    echo ' selected="selected"';
  }
  ?>>PHP 5.2</option>
  <option value="php53"<?php
  if (isset($_POST['listname']) && $_POST
➥['listname'] == 'php53') {
```

```
    echo ' selected="selected"';
  }
  ?>>PHP 5.3</option>
  <option value="php54"><?php
  if (isset($_POST['listname']) &&
➥$_POST['listname'] == 'php54') {
    echo ' selected="selected"';
  }
  ?>>PHP 5.4</option>
</select>
```

On a single selection list, the value of the selected
<option> element is transferred to the server when sub-
mitting the form. This value can then be manually
checked to prefill the form, using the selected HTML
attribute, as shown in the preceding code.

The same effect can be implemented using
getFormData.inc.php; then data from the site's cookies is
used, if available:

```
<?php
  require_once 'getFormData.inc.php';
?>
...
<select name="listname">
  <option value="php52"><?php
  if (getFormDataPOST('listname') == 'php52') {
    echo ' selected="selected"';
  }
  ?>>PHP 5.2</option>
  <option value="php53"><?php
  if (getFormDataPOST('listname') == 'php53') {
    echo ' selected="selected"';
  }
  ?>>PHP 5.3</option>
  <option value="php54"><?php
```

```
  if (getFormDataPOST('listname') == 'php5.4') {
    echo ' selected="selected"';
  }
  ?>>PHP 5.4</option>
</select>
```

Preselecting Multiple Selection Lists

```
<select name="multilistname[]" multiple="multiple"
➥size="3">
  <option value="php52"<?php
  if (isset($_POST['multilistname']) &&
➥is_array($_POST['multilistname']) &&
➥in_array('php52',
$_POST['multilistname'])) {
    echo ' selected="selected"';
  }
  ?>>PHP 5.2</option>
  <option value="php53"<?php
  if (isset($_POST['multilistname']) &&
➥is_array($_POST['multilistname']) &&
➥in_array('php53',
$_POST['multilistname'])) {
    echo ' selected="selected"';
  }
  ?>>PHP 5.3</option>
  <option value="php54"<?php
  if (isset($_POST['multilistname']) &&
➥is_array($_POST['multilistname']) &&
in_array('php54',
$_POST['multilistname'])) {
    echo ' selected="selected"';
  }
  ?>>PHP 5.4</option>
</select>
```

When it comes to prefilling form elements, multiple selection lists are the most difficult ones to implement. This is because in $_GET or $_POST, you have an array of chosen options; so you cannot just compare strings, but you have to search for the specified value in the array. Lucky for us, PHP offers something suitable in the form of the in_array() function. So, the effort required is not much more than with the other form elements: If the current value is in $_GET/$_POST, print out the selected attribute.

However, the HTML form must be specially prepared to allow PHP to access the data from the multiple selection list: The value of the name attribute has to end with [], hinting to PHP that it should expect an array of values, not just a string value. Accessing the list data, however, can still be done using $_GET['listname']/$_POST['listname'] and not $_GET['listname[]']/$_POST['listname[]'], as shown in the preceding code.

If you want to prefill the list with data from the cookie, you just have to use the well-known file getFormData.inc.php from the previous phrases. It contains two additional functions that return an array rather than a string:

```php
function getFormDataArrayGET($name) {
  if (isset($_GET[$name])) {
    return $_GET[$name];
  } else {
    $cookiedata = getCookieData();
    if ($cookiedata != null &&
      isset($cookiedata[$name])) {
      return $cookiedata[$name];
    }
  }
}
```

```php
  return array();
}
function getFormDataArrayPOST($name) {
  if (isset($_POST[$name])) {
    return $_POST[$name];
  } else {
    $cookiedata = getCookieData();
    if ($cookiedata != null &&
      isset($cookiedata[$name])) {
      return $cookiedata[$name];
    }
  }
  return array();
}
```

These functions return an array for multiple lists that
you can use as you did in select-multiple.php:

```php
<?php
  require_once 'getFormData.inc.php';
?>
<!DOCTYPE html PUBLIC "-//W3C//DTD XHTML 1.0
➥Transitional//EN"
"http://www.w3.org/TR/xhtml1/DTD/xhtml1-
➥transitional.dtd">
<html>
<head>
  <title>Forms</title>
</head>
<body>
  <form method="post" action="<?php echo
➥htmlspecialchars($_SERVER['PHP_SELF']); ?>">
    <select name="multilistname[]"
➥multiple="multiple" size="3">
      <option value="php52"><?php
  if (in_array('php52', getFormDataArrayPOST
➥('multilistname'))) {
```

```php
    echo ' selected="selected"';
  }
      ?>>PHP 5.2</option>
      <option value="php53"><?php
  if (in_array('php53', getFormDataArrayPOST
➥('multilistname'))) {
    echo ' selected="selected"';
  }
      ?>>PHP 5.3</option>
      <option value="php54"><?php
  if (in_array('php54', getFormDataArrayPOST
➥('multilistname'))) {
    echo ' selected="selected"';
  }
      ?>>PHP 5.4</option>
    </select><br />
    <input type="submit" />
  </form>
</body>
</html>
```

Processing Graphical Submit Buttons

```php
<?php
  if (isset($_POST['Submit_x']) &&
➥isset($_POST['Submit_y'])) {
    printf('<h1>You clicked at the following
➥coordinates: x-%s, y-%s</h1>',
      htmlspecialchars($_POST['Submit_x']),
      htmlspecialchars($_POST['Submit_y'])
    );
  } else {
?>
```

```
  <form method="post" action="<?php echo
➥htmlspecialchars($_SERVER['PHP_SELF']); ?>">
    <input type="image" name="Submit"
➥src="pearsoned.gif" />
  </form>
<?php
  }
?>
```

Graphical Submit buttons (`<input type="image" />`) are
not only a nice way to spice up the layout of the form,
but they also offer a nice feature: The browser submits
the x and the y coordinates of the mouse pointer when
clicking the button. In PHP, this happens by appending
_x and _y to the name attribute of the button and writ-
ing this into $_GET or $_POST. The preceding code evaluates this information.

NOTE: When you submit the form using the keyboard
(for example, with the Enter key), both coordinates
are 0.

Checking Mandatory Fields

```
<?php
  if (isset($_POST['Submit']) &&
      isset($_POST['textfieldname']) &&
      trim($_POST['textfieldname']) != '') {
    echo '<h1>Thank you for filling out this
➥form!</h1>';
  } else {
?>
  <form method="post" action="<?php echo
➥htmlspecialchars($_SERVER['PHP_SELF']); ?>">
```

```
    <input type="text" name="textfieldname"
      value="<?php
  echo (isset($_POST['textfieldname'])) ?
➥htmlspecialchars($_POST['textfieldname']) : '';
      ?>" />
    <input type="submit" name="Submit" />
  </form>
<?php
  }
?>
```

During form validation, the emphasis is on mandatory fields most of the time. You can check whether they contain values in two ways:

- Check whether the fields exist in $_GET/$_POST:

```
if (!isset($_GET['fieldname'])) {
  // Error!
}
```

- Check whether the values in $_GET/$_POST contain information other than whitespace:

```
if (trim($_GET['fieldname') == '') {
  // Error!
}
```

It is very important that you combine *both* techniques. You always have to check for a field's existence using isset() to avoid error messages when trying to access array values that do not exist. But, because text fields are always submitted, you always have to check whether there is something within the field apart from whitespace. In addition, when empty, isset() always returns true independent of the field's value. The code at the beginning of this phrase shows an example.

TIP: This methodology also applies for all other text form elements, radio buttons, and check boxes. It can be easily extended to check for certain patterns, including valid email addresses. See Chapter 2, "Working with Arrays," for phrases that can be of assistance here.

NOTE: The code for prefilling the form element has been left intact so that this code snippet can be merged with other code snippets. So, if the form has only partially been filled out, the correct form fields are prefilled.

Checking Selection Lists

```php
<?php
  if (isset($_POST['Submit']) &&
      isset($_POST['listname']) &&
      $_POST['listname'] != '') {
    echo '<h1>Thank you for filling out this
➥form!</h1>';
  } else {
?>
  <form method="post" action="<?php echo
➥htmlspecialchars($_SERVER['PHP_SELF']); ?>">
    <select name="listname">
      <option value="">Please select from
➥list</option>
      <option value="php52"<?php
  if (isset($_POST['listname']) &&
$_POST['listname'] == 'php52') {
    echo ' selected="selected"';
  }
```

```
    ?>>PHP 5.2</option>
    <option value="php53"<?php
if (isset($_POST['listname']) && $_POST
➥['listname'] == 'php53') {
  echo ' selected="selected"';
}
    ?>>PHP 5.3</option>
    <option value="php54"<?php
if (isset($_POST['listname']) && $_POST
➥['listname'] == 'php54') {
  echo ' selected="selected"';
}
    ?>>PHP 5.4</option>
  </select><br />
  <input type="submit" name="Submit" />
</form>
<?php
  }
?>
```

When it comes to validating a selection list, the
approach depends on the type of list:

- If it is a list in which only one element may be
  selected, the list is considered to be filled out
  incorrectly if

    - No option in the list is selected.

    - The selected option has an empty string as a
      value.

- If it is a list in which multiple elements may be
  selected, the list is considered to be filled out
  incorrectly if

    - No option in the list is selected.

    - All selected options have an empty string as a
      value.

Options with empty strings as values come into play if the list contains functionless dummy entries that have captions such as "Please choose from list." These list options must not receive a value other than "", so that the validation algorithm can distinguish these entries from reasonable ones.

The listing at the beginning of this phrase validates a single selection list—again including PHP code to pre-fill the list.

With multiple lists, a bit more work is required, as shown in the following code. If the form has been submitted, the array of selected list elements is searched. If one element that is nonempty is found, the process is complete and the user can be congratulated for the successful completion of the form. Otherwise, the form is displayed again:

```php
<?php
  $ok = false;
  if (isset($_POST['Submit']) &&
      isset($_POST['multilistname'])) {
    if (is_array($_POST['multilistname'])) {
      for ($i=0; $i < count(
➥$_POST['multilistname']); $i++) {
        if ($_POST['multilistname'][$i] != '') {
          $ok = true;
          break;
        }
      }
    }
  }

  if ($ok) {
    echo '<h1>Thank you for filling out this
➥form!</h1>';
```

```
  } else {
?>
  <form method="post" action="<?php echo
➥htmlspecialchars($_SERVER['PHP_SELF']); ?>">
    <select name="multilistname[]"
➥multiple="multiple" size="3">

    </select>
<br />
    <input type="submit" name="Submit" />
  </form>
<?php
  }
?>
```

Escaping Output

```
filter_input(INPUT_POST, 'fieldName',
➥FILTER_SANITIZE_SPECIAL_CHARS);
```

Escaping output is one of the key pillars of secure web development. If you output dynamic data (that is, information provided by the client or any other untrusted external source), you need to escape special characters based on the context in which you output the data. Usually, the context is HTML, so you need to escape special characters in HTML—", ', <, >, and &. PHP provides the htmlspecialchars() function for this task, but the filter extension which was added in PHP 5.2 offers a more generic approach.

The filter_input() function does not mandatorily filter input, but may also help in escaping special characters. As a first argument, you provide where to look for data to be filtered (for example, INPUT_POST for POST data and INPUT_GET for GET data). In the second function

argument, you provide the name of the GET/POST/...
variable to be taken care of. In the third argument, you
provide the filter to use. The following code generates a
list of all filters and their numeric IDs that can be used
for filter_input():

```
$list = filter_list();
foreach ($list as $value) {
  printr('%s: %s', $value, filter_id($value));
}
```

PHP also has built-in constants for all filters (for
example, FILTER_SANITIZE_SPECIAL_CHARS instead of its
numeric value, 515).

NOTE: You can escape variables, as well. Just use
filter_var() instead of filter_input() and provide
the variable and the filter to use.

Validating Input

```
$email = filter_input(INPUT_POST, 'email',
➥FILTER_VALIDATE_EMAIL);
```

Not only support filter_input() and filter_var()
functions (and their sibling functions) the escaping
of data, but also a validation of data (for example,
whether a variable or form field contains a valid email
address). These validation filters are easy to spot when
the built-in PHP constants are used—for instance,
FILTER_VALIDATE_EMAIL. Other validation constants
are FILTER_VALIDATE_REGEXP, FILTER_VALIDATE_URL, and
FILTER_VALIDATE_IP.

The return values of those validations may be a bit surprising, but they are aligning with the return valid of the other filters: The validated (in this case, unchanged) data is returned. If a validation fails, however, the functions return `false`. So, after validating the input or the variable, you either have good data or no data.

Writing All Form Data into a File

```php
<?php
  if (isset($_POST['Submit']) &&
      isset($_POST['fieldname']) &&
      trim($_POST['fieldname']) != '') {
    echo '<h1>Thank you for filling out this
➥form!</h1>';
    $data = '';
    $data = @file_get_contents('formdata.txt');
    if ($data != '') {
      $data = unserialize($data);
    }
    $data[] = $_POST;
    file_put_contents('formdata.txt',
➥serialize($data));
  } else {
?>
  <form method="post" action="<?php echo
➥htmlspecialchars($_SERVER['PHP_SELF']); ?>">
  ...
  </form>
<?php
  }
?>
```

After a user fills out a form correctly, what do you do with the form data? A very intuitive approach that does not require too much setup on the server is to write the data into a file on the server.

The preceding code contains a very naïve approach: All data is stored in a file on the server. When the form is submitted, the file is read in and unserialized into an array. Then, the form data is appended to the array. Finally, the array is serialized again and written back to the file.

Figure 5.3 shows this file in a text editor.

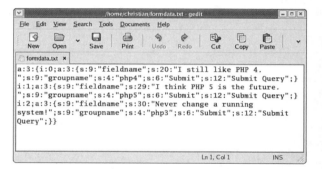

Figure 5.3   Data written into the form (but which can later be unserialized)

NOTE: Of course, race conditions could occur, and the file could be simultaneously read by two processes, which would result in just one of the two processes appearing in the file. To avoid this, you have to implement file locking as shown in Chapter 7.

Sending All Form Data via Email

```php
<?php
  if (isset($_POST['Submit']) &&
      isset($_POST['fieldname']) &&
      trim($_POST['fieldname']) != '' &&
      $_POST['groupname'] != '') {
    echo '<h1>Thank you for filling out this
form!</h1>';
    $text = '';
    foreach ($_POST as $name => $value) {
      if (is_array($value)) {
        $text .= sprintf("%s: %s\n", $name, join('
', $value));
      } else {
        $text .= sprintf("%s: %s\n", $name, $value);
      }
    }
    mail('recipient@example.com', 'Form data',
$text);
  } else {
?>
  <form method="post" action="<?php echo
htmlspecialchars($_SERVER['PHP_SELF']); ?>">
  ...
  </form>
<?php
  }
?>
```

A more imminent notification of someone filling out a
form can be implemented by sending form data via
email. Of course, you can write a custom mail script
for each and every form; however, the preceding code
shows how this can be done universally. Via for, all

form data is merged into a string. Special care is taken of form values that are arrays—this can occur with multiple selection lists. Then the form data is mailed to the webmaster; just don't forget to change the email address.

Getting Information about File Uploads

```php
<?php
  if (isset($_POST['Submit']) &&
      isset($_FILES['File']) &&
      is_uploaded_file($_FILES['tmp_name'])) {
    printf('<p>Error: %s<br />
            Original name: %s<br />
            File size: %s<br />
            Temporary name: %s<br />
            MIME type: %s</p>',
      $_FILES['File']['error'],
      htmlspecialchars($_FILES['File']['name']),
      $_FILES['File']['size'],
      $_FILES['File']['tmp_name'],
      htmlspecialchars($_FILES['File']['type'])
    );
  } else {
?>
  <form action="<?php echo $_SERVER['PHP_SELF']; ?>"
    method="post" enctype="multipart/form-data">
    <input type="file" name="File" />
    <input type="submit" name="Submit" value="Submit
➥form" />
  </form>
<?php
  }
?>
```

When you are uploading files to the Web server using `<input type="file" />`, the HTML form has to fulfill two requirements:

- The `enctype` attribute has to be set to `"multipart/form-data"`.

- The `method` attribute has to be set to `"post"`.

Without these settings, the file upload does not work. It also does not work if the following information is missing from `php.ini`:

```
file_uploads = On
```

But if it does, retrieving information about the file is quite easy: In the (superglobal) array `$_FILES`, you can find the file upload form field under its name. Then, the following subkeys provide further information about the uploaded file:

- **`$_FILES["File"]["error"]`**—Error code (0 in case of success)

- **`$_FILES["File"]["name"]`**—Original filename

- **`$_FILES["File"]["size"]`**—Size of the file

- **`$_FILES["File"]["tmp_name"]`**—Temporary filename where PHP saved the file

- **`$_FILES["File"]["type"]`**—The file's MIME type as sent by the client, not reliable

The preceding code outputs the available file information (see Figure 5.4). The call to `is_uploaded_file()` adds an additional layer of security by first checking whether the file has really been uploaded by the client.

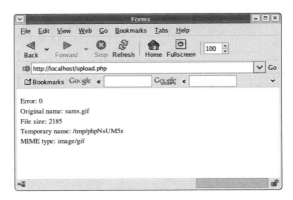

Figure 5.4   Information about the uploaded file

NOTE: Some caveats apply when working with form fields. There is the possibility to provide a maximum file length for the uploaded files in a hidden form field; however, this check is then executed server side, so it is definitely better if you do that on your own in your script, using the "type" array subelement.

Also, do not rely on the "name" array subelement because this information (the original filename) can be forged. Even worse, some browsers do not always send the original filename, but the complete path to it. Therefore, always call basename() to extract the file-name only.

In our code, we run htmlspecialchars() before out-putting any of these two pieces of information.

Moving Uploaded Files to a Safe Location

```php
<?php
  if (isset($_POST['Submit']) &&
      isset($_FILES['File'])) {
    $move = move_uploaded_file(
      $_FILES['File']['tmp_name'],
      '/tmp/' . basename($_FILES['File']['name'])
    );
    echo '<h1>';
    echo ($move) ? 'Moved' : 'Did not move';
    echo ' the file!</h1>';
  } else {
?>
  <form action="<?php echo $_SERVER['PHP_SELF']; ?>"
    method="post" enctype="multipart/form-data">
    <input type="file" name="File" />
    <input type="submit" name="Submit" value="Submit
➥form" />
  </form>
<?php
  }
?>
```

When a user uploads a file to a PHP script using the
<input type="file" /> HTML element, PHP stores the
file in a temporary location (set in the php.ini directive
upload_tmp_dir) and deletes it upon completion of
script execution. Therefore, you have to access the
uploaded file within the script. To do so, PHP contains
the function move_uploaded_file(), which moves a file
from one location to another. The great thing about
move_uploaded_file() is that the function first does a

sanity check, whether the filename you provide really is an uploaded file or if a malicious user just tried to trick you into moving /etc/passwd or C:\boot.ini somewhere else.

Suppose the path /tmp exists and is writable by the Web server and the PHP process. In this case, the preceding code moves the uploaded file to this directory, using its original filename (and you do not care whether the filename already exists).

Monitoring the Progress of a File Upload

```
var_dump($_SESSION[ini_get('session.upload_progress_
➥prefix') . 'myUpload');
?>
```

As of the time of writing, web browsers do not contain built-in functionality to determine the status of a file upload. Especially with large files or slow connections, this information would be very valuable.

Most Web applications today that do show how much of a file has already been uploaded use a plug-in technology such as Flash, Silverlight, or Java. Starting with PHP version 5.4, it is also possible to determine the status of a file upload with server-side means.

The php.ini file contains configuration options for the file upload status feature. These are the most important options:

- **session.upload_progress.enabled**—Activates file upload tracking, must be set to On.

- **session.upload_progress.prefix**—Key prefix in
  the $_SESSION array where file upload status infor-
  mation will be stored. Defaults to
  upload_progress_.

- **session.upload_progress.name**—Name of the POST
  value, which will contain the key suffix in the
  $_SESSION array where file upload status informa-
  tion will be stored. Defaults to
  PHP_SESSION_UPLOAD_PROGRESS.

Normally when you use this feature, you include some
JavaScript code that continuously calls a server script to
find out the update status. For the sake of brevity, we
use a much simpler approach here.

In one file, we set up a file upload. PHP automatically
stores file upload information in the session if the following two conditions are met:

- The form must contain a (ideally hidden) form
  field with the name equaling the
  session.upload_progress.prefix value.

- The PHP session must have been started.

Here is a typical form:

```php
<?php
  session_start();
?>
<form method="post" action=""
     enctype="multipart/form-data">
  <input type="file" name="upload" />
  <input type="hidden"
   name="<?php echo
➥ini_get('session.upload_progress.name'); ?>"
   value="<?php echo session_id(); ?>" />
  <input type="submit" value="Upload" />
</form>
```

The hidden form field could then look like that—of course, depending on the php.ini settings and the current session ID:

```
<input type="hidden"
 name="PHP_SESSION_UPLOAD_PROGRESS"
 value="ktgbht0abtnb897fv3j4prl6g6" />
```

Then, when the user submits the form and thus uploads the file,
`$_SESSION['upload_progress_ktgbht0abtnb897fv3j4prl6g6']` contains information about the file upload in form of an array, including the start time, the total number of bytes expected by the server, and how much of that has already been transferred from the client. The name of the `$_SESSION` key is generated by the `session.upload_progress.prefix` value and the value in the hidden form field.

For testing purposes, you might want to open up a PHP file in another tab that continuously outputs the data in that `$_SESSION` field. Figure 5.5 shows a possible output.

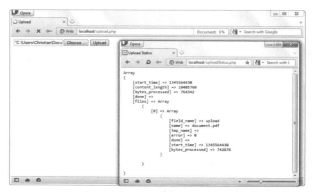

Figure 5.5   Determining the status of an HTTP file upload

NOTE: During testing, we found that this feature does not work on all servers. Especially on Windows systems, the $_SESSION feature remained empty. We are confident that this will work better in future versions of PHP.

What Does PEAR Offer?

The following PHP Extension and Application Repository (PEAR) packages offer functionality helpful for processing form data of any kind:

- HTML_QuickForm2 is a very convenient package to create forms using an object-oriented programming syntax and includes very mighty validation and processing features.
- HTTP_Upload helps to manage file uploads and offers advanced features such as providing valid extensions for uploads. However, the package is unmaintained as of time of writing.

6

Remembering Users (Cookies and Sessions)

Hypertext Transfer Protocol (HTTP) is a stateless protocol. Put simply, a client (Web browser) connects to a Web server, sends a request, and gets a response. Then, the connection is closed. The consequence is the next time the same client sends a request to the same Web server, it is a new request, so the Web server cannot identify the caller. This is, of course, a problem for applications in which state must be maintained (for instance, e-commerce applications with a shopping-cart functionality).

However, you can overcome this limitation in several ways. The basic idea is to send some information with the HTTP response; to try to achieve that, this information is sent back with all subsequent requests to that server. The following possibilities exist:

- Sending the data via POST (that is, a form is required each time)

- Sending the data via GET (that is, by appending this information to the request's uniform resource locator [URL])

- Sending the data as part of the HTTP header (in the form of a cookie)

In real-world projects, one of two methods is used: sessions (via GET or cookies) and cookies.

Understanding Cookies

A cookie is sent as part of the HTTP header and is basically a name-value pair. Their main disadvantage is it is possible to deactivate cookies in the Web browser (and also to filter them out in proxy servers). Some people think cookies create privacy issues. Part of this might have been caused by an article written by John Udell in March 1997, in which he wrote that every cookie can be read from every Web server, thus there is no privacy. This caused quite a stir, although, unfortunately, the correction two months later did not get that amount of attention.

The fact is that cookies have some limitations:

- Cookies are tied to domains, usually the domain that sent the cookie.

- Cookies can be tied to paths on the Web server.

- A cookie contains only text information, 4096 bytes at max (including the cookie name and the = character between the name and value).

- Browsers must only accept up to 20 cookies per domain and 300 cookies in total (although some browsers accept more).

NOTE: The (unofficial) cookie specification goes back to Netscape and has been archived at http://curl.haxx.se/rfc/cookie_spec.html. There have been attempts to create a special Request For Comment (RFC) for next-generation cookies, but this hasn't found any reasonable browser support yet.

Cookies are sent as part of the HTTP header. If a cookie is set, the HTTP header entry `Set-Cookie` is created. The name and value of the cookie (both strings) follow and, optionally, further information such as expiration date, domain, and path of the cookie. For instance, when visiting www.php.net/, the PHP Web site sends this header entry. (Your mileage may vary, especially in terms of the language and IP address used.)

```
Set-Cookie: COUNTRY=DEU%2C84.154.17.84; expires=Thu,
17-May-12 15:23:29 GMT; path=/; domain=.php.net
```

When the browser (or the user) accepts the cookie, it is then sent back to the server in the HTTP header `Cookie:`

```
Cookie: COUNTRY=DEU%2C84.154.17.84
```

TIP: To actually see the HTTP headers, you could use special extensions to standard Web browsers. For Mozilla browsers (including Firefox), the LiveHTTPHeaders extension available at http://livehttpheaders.mozdev.org/ is a real time-saver. Users of Microsoft Internet Explorer might be interested in installing ieHTTPHeaders, an Explorer bar available from www.blunck.info/iehttpheaders.html. The built-in Web

development add-ins of many modern browser also provide easy access to cookie information. Figure 6.1
shows some of the output the Firefox extension shows
when accessing the PHP home page.

Figure 6.1   Cookies are set as part of the HTTP header.

A cookie can have an expiration date. If that is set, the
cookie lives up to this date (at most) and is a so-called
persistent cookie. After that, the browser automatically
deletes the cookie—but this could also happen earlier
(for example, when the maximum number of cookies
in the browser is reached and the oldest cookies are
purged). If no cookie expiration date is set, however, a
so-called session cookie or temporary cookie has been
created. This lives as long as the Web browser is running. When it is closed, the cookie is deleted.

Creating a Cookie

`setcookie()`

```php
<?php
  setcookie('version', phpversion());
?>
Tried to send cookie.
```

Setting a Cookie (setcookie.php)

To create a cookie, the PHP function `setcookie()` can be used. It expects the following parameters; however, only the first one is mandatory:

- The name of the cookie
- The value of the cookie
- The expiry date (in UNIX epoch format)
- The path on the Web server from which the cookie may be accessed
- The domain from which the cookie may be accessed
- Whether the cookie may only be sent using secure (HTTP Secure [HTTPS]/Secure Sockets Layer [SSL]) connections
- Whether the cookie shall only be accessible by the server after an HTTP request, but shall be hidden from JavaScript

The preceding code sets a simple session cookie with the current PHP version as its value.

TIP

The last two options of `setcookie()` can be important security safeguards. By limiting cookies to HTTPS connections it is harder to "sniff" cookie data (like session IDs) in open networks. And if JavaScript does not have access to cookie information, some attack vectors may cease to exist.

Figure 6.2 shows a cookie warning in the Firefox browser. You can clearly see the cookie name and script.

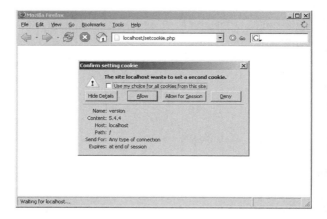

Figure 6.2   Firefox receives the cookie and asks the user what to do.

WARNING: Because cookies are sent as part of the HTTP header, they have to be created before any Hypertext Markup Language (HTML) content is sent out (unless you are using output buffering). Otherwise, you receive an error message such as the one shown in Figure 6.3.

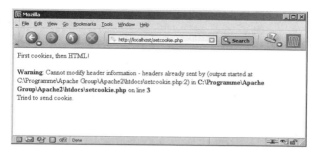

Figure 6.3 Cookies have to be sent prior to any HTML content.

NOTE: Usually, PHP takes care of escaping special characters in the cookie values (in URL format). However, it is possible to do this manually by sending raw cookie data. For this, the function `setrawcookie()` accepts the same parameter as `setcookie()`, but does not encode the cookie's value. You must do that manually, with the function `urlencode()`.

Reading Out Cookies

```php
<table>
<?php
  foreach ($_COOKIE as $name => $value) {
    printf('<tr><td>%s</td><td>%s</td></tr>',
      htmlspecialchars($name),
      htmlspecialchars($value));
  }
?>
</table>
```

Reading Out Cookies (getcookie.php)

All cookies to which the server has access (not all cookies that are stored in the browser!) are available in the superglobal array $_COOKIE. The foreach loop reads in all cookies and sends them to the client in an HTML table.

Setting a (Reasonable) Expiry Date

```php
<?php
  setcookie('version', phpversion(), time() +
➥21*24*60*60);
?>
Tried to send cookie.
```

Setting a Cookie with a Relative Expiry Date (setcookie-expiry.php)

The expiry date of a cookie is the third parameter for setcookie(). It is an integer value; therefore, the epoch value for a time stamp must be used. Chapter 3, "Date and Time," contains quite a lot of information on how to work with this type of information.

Usually, it is a good thing to set a relative expiry date for a cookie ("in three weeks") rather than an absolute date ("end of May 2012"). If you use absolute dates, you might have to change your script on a regular basis because the absolute expiry date might arrive soon. It is also considered very unprofessional to set expiry dates that are in the very distant future, for instance in the year 2030. The client that receives this cookie will most certainly not be booted any more in that year.

Therefore, use a relative date. The PHP function `time()` retrieves the current epoch value; then add to this the number of seconds you want the cookie to live. The code at the beginning of this phrase sets a cookie that will exist for three weeks.

Setting a Client-Specific Expiry Date

```
setcookie('version', phpversion(),
    $_GET['time'] + 21*24*60*60)
```

```php
<?php
  if (isset($_GET['time']) && is_int($_GET['time']))
➡{
    setcookie('version', phpversion(),
      $_GET['time'] + 21*24*60*60);
  } else {
    setcookie('version', phpversion(),
      time() + 21*24*60*60);
  }
?>
Tried to send cookie.
```

*Setting a Cookie with a Specific Expiry Date
(setcookie-specific.php)*

Keep in mind that the decision of when a cookie expires is made on the client side, using the client time settings. So, if the client has the wrong date (which is something you cannot control from the server side), your cookies might expire sooner than you expect. So, don't try to set cookies that live for just one hour or so; small things like daylight savings time (DST) could destroy your plan.

However, with a bit of JavaScript, it can be possible to avoid this trap. The code in the following listing is client-side JavaScript code that determines the current time (client side) as an epoch value and sends it to a server-side script, setcookie-specific.php. The main difference between PHP's time() function and JavaScript's getTime() method is that the latter returns the number of milliseconds since January 1, 1970, whereas the former just works with the number of seconds. So, the JavaScript value first has to be divided by 1,000 and rounded down.

The code for this file can be seen at the beginning of this phrase: The transmitted value is taken as the basis for the calculation of the relative cookie expiration date:

```
<script type="text/javascript">
  var epoch = (new Date()).getTime();
  epoch = Math.floor(epoch / 1000);
  location.replace("setcookie-specific.php?time=" +
➥epoch);
</script>
```

Using JavaScript to Transfer the Local Time Information to the Server (setcookie-specific.html; excerpt)

Deleting a Cookie

```
setcookie('version', '', time() - 10*365*24*60*60);
```

```
<?php
  setcookie('version', '', time() -
➥10*365*24*60*60);
?>
Tried to delete cookie.
```

Deleting a Cookie (deletecookie.php)

An intuitive way to delete a cookie is to set its value to an empty string. However, the cookie is still there, albeit without a value. A better way is to additionally send a cookie with the same name again, but provide an expiry date that is in the past. Again, incorrect local time settings have to be taken into account, so use a really small expiry date (for instance, ten years before today). This listing implements this and deletes the version cookie that has been sent by the previous listings. Here, both methods are combined: The cookie value is set to an empty string, and the expiry date is in the past. Figure 6.4 shows the result: The browser tries to delete the cookie by setting the expiry date to the current time; so, in the next second, it is gone.

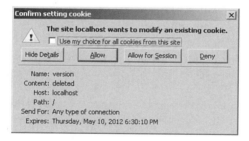

Figure 6.4   The cookie will be deleted (if the user accepts it).

WARNING: If you try to set the expiration date to 0, PHP just skips this parameter; so, this does not work. You do have to provide a positive parameter, even if it's 1.

Making Cookies Accessible for Several Domains

```
setcookie('version', phpversion(), 0,
➥'.example.com');
```

```php
<?php
  setcookie('version', phpversion(), 0,
➥'.example.com');
?>
Tried to send cookie.
```

Setting the Domain for a Cookie (setcookie-domain.php)

One part of the Set-Cookie header sent by a server is the domain that has access to this cookie. If not sent specifically, this value defaults to the domain that is sending the cookie. Setting this domain to a completely different value (for example, the domain of an ad server [so-called third-party cookies; used to try to generate a profile of the user]) does not always work because many browsers allow users to specifically disable that. (Figure 6.5 shows an example in the Netscape 4.x browser, which, even back in its "pre-historic" heyday, was capable of blocking cookies that didn't use the originating domain.)

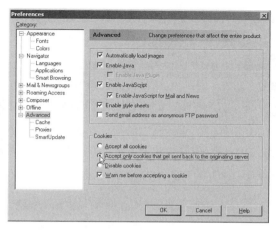

Figure 6.5   Even Netscape 4.x allows you to block cookies that do not use the originating domain.

Sometimes, however, the use of cookies is required on third-level domains or subdomains (for instance, www.example.com, store.example.com, and ssl.example.com). Large Web sites with many subdomains, such as Amazon and eBay, require that all top-level domains (TLDs) are supported. To achieve this, the domain of the cookie—fourth parameter of setcookie()—has to be set. Here comes the trick: All domain names are valid, as long as they contain two dots. So, if you set the domain to .example.com, all third-level domains of example.com have access to this cookie. There is one *but*: Pages on http://example.com/ cannot access this cookie. So, you might want to try to set the domain to example.com; however, this does not conform with the specification and might not be supported in all browsers.

Checking Whether the Client Supports Cookies

```
$test_temp = isset($_COOKIE['test_temp']) ?
    'supports' : 'does not support';
$test_persist = isset($_COOKIE['test_persist']) ?
    'supports' : 'does not support';
```

```php
<?php
  if (isset($_GET['step']) && $_GET['step'] == '2')
➥{
    $test_temp = isset($_COOKIE['test_temp']) ?
      'supports' : 'does not support';
    $test_persist = isset($_COOKIE['test_persist'])
➥?
      'supports' : 'does not support';
    setcookie('test_temp', '', time() -
➥365*24*60*60);
    setcookie('test_persist', '', time() -
➥365*24*60*60);
    echo "Browser $test_temp temporary cookies.<br
➥/>";
    echo "Browser $test_persist persistent
➥cookies.";
  } else {
    setcookie('test_temp', 'ok');
    setcookie('test_persist', 'ok', time() +
➥14*24*60*60);
    header("Location:
{$_SERVER['PHP_SELF']}?step=2");
  }
?>
```

Testing the Cookie Configuration of a Browser (cookietest.php)

Remember the way cookies are sent: First, the server sends the cookie to the client as part of the HTTP response. In the next request, the client sends the cookie back if accepted. Therefore, calling setcookie() and then checking the contents of $_COOKIE does *not* work. You have to wait for the next HTTP request.

You can, however, use header() to force the client to create a second request. In the first request, you set the cookie; in the second request, you check whether that worked.

In the preceding code, two cookies are set, one temporary cookie and one persistent cookie—because it is possible to configure some browsers so that one kind of cookie is accepted, the other one is not. Then, the redirect is done using header() and the Location: HTTP header, and the presence of the cookies is checked.

Of course, you should configure your browser to show a message window when a cookie arrives; that makes debugging much easier.

Saving Multiple Data in One Cookie

```
setcookie('cookiedata', serialize($cookiedata))
```

```php
<?php
  function setCookieData($arr) {
    $cookiedata = getAllCookieData();
    if ($cookiedata == null) {
      $cookiedata = array();
    }
    foreach ($arr as $name => $value) {
      $cookiedata[$name] = $value;
    }
    setcookie('cookiedata',
```

```
      serialize($cookiedata),
      time() + 30*24*60*60);
  }

function getAllCookieData() {
  if (isset($_COOKIE['cookiedata'])) {
    $formdata = $_COOKIE['cookiedata'];
    if ($formdata != '') {
      return unserialize($formdata);
    } else {
      return array();
    }
  } else {
    return null;
  }
}

function getCookieData($name) {
  $cookiedata = getAllCookieData();
  if ($cookiedata != null &&
    isset($cookiedata[$name])) {
      return $cookiedata[$name];
  }
}
  return '';
}
?>
```

Helper Library to Save Multiple Values into One Cookie
(getCookieData.inc.php)

Usually, one cookie has one value: one string.
Therefore, to store multiple data in cookies, multiple
cookies have to be used. This, however, could create

some problems (for instance, the limit of 20 cookies per domain). Therefore, it might make sense to try to save multiple data in one cookie. For this, an array comes in handy. Just remember that cookies can only contain strings, so we need to use serialization to prepare the data.

For this, you can write a library that is quite similar to the library used in the Chapter 2, "Working with Arrays," to save form data in a cookie. One cookie called cookiedata contains all values as an associative array. The function getCookieData() returns one specific value, whereas setCookieData() takes an array and writes its contents to the cookie. The preceding listing shows the complete code for this library.

The following listing uses this library to implement the cookie test from the previous phrase using this library:

```php
<?php
  require_once 'getCookieData.inc.php';

  if (isset($_GET['step']) && $_GET['step'] == '2')
  {
    $test = (getCookieData('test') == 'ok') ?
      'supports' : 'does not support';
    echo "Browser $test cookies.";
  } else {
    setCookieData(array('test' => 'ok'));
    header("Location:
{$_SERVER['PHP_SELF']}?step=2");
  }
?>
```

Testing the Cookie Configuration of a Browser—Using the Helper Library (cookietest-serialize.php)

Saving the User's Language Preference

```
setcookie('lang', $_SERVER['PHP_SELF'], time() +
➥30*24*60*60, '/')
```

```php
<?php
  if (!isset($_COOKIE['lang']) ||
    $_COOKIE['lang'] != $_SERVER['PHP_SELF']) {
    setcookie('lang', $_SERVER['PHP_SELF'],
      time() + 30*24*60*60, '/');
  }
?>
```

Saving the Current Path in a Cookie (saveLanguage.inc.php)

Many Web pages are multilingual. In addition, they are often organized so that every localized section resides in its own directory, similar to this approach:

- The English language version resides in the en directory.
- The Spanish language version resides in the es directory.
- The French language version resides in the fr directory.

You can detect the language of the user in several different ways:

- By trying to tie the client's IP address to a geographic region
- By reading the Accept-Language HTTP header to determine which languages are the preferred ones
- By asking the user

Although all of these methods work somehow, the last one (or a combination of several of them) is considered to be most user friendly. So, you do need a home page that offers links to all three versions. That's simple HTML, as shown here:

```
<a href="en/index.php">English version</a><br />
<a href="es/index.php">Versión español</a><br />
<a href="fr/index.php">Versione française</a>
```

Home Page Linking to the Various Language Versions (multilingual.php; excerpt)

Now, every language directory has an `index.php` file in the specific language. In this file, the code is included from the listing at the beginning of this phrase. This checks whether there is already a language cookie. If not, it tries to set a cookie with the current path (retrieved from `$_SERVER['PHP_SELF']`).

NOTE: It is important to set the cookie's path to the root directory of the Web server. Otherwise, the path defaults to the current path, and the cookie is automatically only readable in the current directory and its sub-directories, and not on the home page.

Finally, you have to check on the home page to determine whether the cookie is present, and, if so, redirect the user to the appropriate page. To do so, you must add the following code at the top of the `multilingual.php` page:

```
<?php
  if (isset($_COOKIE['lang']) && $_COOKIE['lang'] !=
➥'') {
```

```
    header("Location: {$_COOKIE['lang']}");
  }
?>
```

Checking for the Language Cookie (multilingual.php; excerpt)

Understanding Sessions

Originally, a session is a visit of a user to a Web site. He clicks a few links, has a look at a couple of pages, and then leaves. This defines a session. In other words, if a user does not request any data from a Web site for a period of time (for example, 20 minutes), the session ends.

HTTP does not know any kind of session mechanism; the protocol is stateless. However, PHP comes with a built-in session support that makes it fairly easy to use sessions.

After a session is created, PHP generates a session ID (that is, a long string that identifies the session). PHP then creates a file or a database entry for this session. Then, the PHP application can store data in this session. This data is then written either into the session file or into the database. (Shared memory is another, but rarely used option.)

So, the only thing that must be transported between the client and the server is the session ID. All other data relevant to the session resides at the server. So, no sensitive data is sent over the wire an unnecessary number of times.

The configuration of PHP's session mechanism is completely triggered in the [session] section of the php.ini configuration file. The default settings might not be suitable for all applications, so the next few phrases cover some possible configurations.

Where to Store the Sessions

Usually, session data is stored in files. The location of these files is set in the php.ini directive session.save_path. Of course, this path must (a) exist and (b) be readable and writable for the PHP process (usually, the process of the Web server). Otherwise, the session information cannot be stored.

However, when you have a lot of users and, therefore, a lot of sessions, PHP should not put all session files in one directory because this might cause some serious performance issues. The following syntax allows PHP to move session data into many subdirectories:

```
session.save_path = "n;/tmp"
```

This creates subdirectories up to the level of n within the /tmp directory. However, these subdirectories have to exist so that PHP's session mechanism can write into them; for this, there exists the shell script mod_files.sh in the ext/session directory.

Of course, only the Web server should be allowed to read this directory; otherwise, other users in the system could be able to read session information with possibly sensitive data.

How to Maintain the Session State

The session ID has to be sent to the browser with every response and—much more important—has to be sent back to the server with every request.

The easiest way to do so is to use cookies. PHP then sends a cookie with the name PHPSESSID (can be changed with the directive session.name) to the client. However, for this to happen, the following php.ini directive must be set:

```
session.use_cookies = 1
```

However, what happens if the client does not support cookies? Then, a second mechanism comes into play, in the form of the following directive:

```
session.use_trans_sid = 0
```

Then, PHP automatically falls back into a mode in which the session ID is appended automatically to all URLs. This could create some potential security risks (session fixation and session hijacking, for example). Most well-known e-commerce Web sites stopped using this mechanism (for instance, Amazon). When no personal data is stored in a session, you might want to use this feature nevertheless.

To be able to use session.user_trans_sid, PHP must be compiled with the switch –enable-trans-sid, something that is automatically done for the Windows and Mac OS X binaries.

The other option is to allow only cookies, not session IDs, in uniform resource locators (URLs). To do so, you can use the following php.ini directive:

```
session.use_only_cookies = 1
```

NOTE: Session IDs in the URL are generally a bad thing. For example, because people could bookmark this information, some search engines will not include your sites if they include such. Nearly every major e-commerce Web site requires cookies nowadays.

Activating Sessions

`session_start()`

```php
<?php
  session_start();
  echo 'Sessions activated.';
?>
```

Activating Sessions (session_start.php)

Using session management always requires resources and, therefore, costs performance. So, sessions have to be activated. Because cookies might be part of the package, this has to be done before any HTML content is sent to the client. This can be accomplished in two ways:

- Activate sessions globally with the `php.ini` directive `session.auto_start = 1`.
- Activate sessions on a per-script basis with the function `session_start()`.

From a performance point of view, the latter option is the best one.

Reading and Writing Sessions

```php
<?php
  session_start();
  echo 'Sessions activated.<br />';
  $_SESSION['version'] = phpversion();
  echo 'Session data written.<br />';
  echo "Session data read: {$_SESSION['version']}.";
➥//could also be used on another page
?>
```

Reading and Writing Sessions (session_readwrite.php)

All session data is accessible from a PHP script via the
$_SESSION array. Because the data itself is stored on the
server side, you can write session data and read it in the
next PHP statement, without the requirement of a
round-trip to the server as it was with cookies. Just
remember to call session_start() first and then access
$_SESSION. The preceding listing creates a session file
that Figure 6.6 shows.

Figure 6.6   The content of the session file created
from the preceding code.

Closing Sessions

`session_destroy()`

```php
<?php
  session_start();
  echo 'Before: <pre>';
  print_r($_SESSION);
  echo '</pre>After: <pre> ';
  session_destroy();
  print_r($_SESSION);
  echo '</pre>';
?>
```

Removing All Session Data (session_destroy.php)

In some instances (for example, when a user logs out), all session data should be removed, and the session must be closed. Of course, it is possible to loop through $_SESSION with foreach and then set each value to an empty string or null, but there is a quicker way: Call session_destroy(). After that, all data in the current session is destroyed, as the function name suggests.

Changing the Session ID

`session_regenerate_id()`

```php
<?php
  ob_start();
  session_start();
  echo 'Old: ' . session_id();
  session_regenerate_id();
```

```
  echo '<br />New: ' . session_id();
  ob_end_flush();
?>
```

Changing the Session ID (session_regenerate_id.php)

One common attack against Web sites that are secured
with sessions is that the session ID of a user is somehow taken (for instance, by analyzing HTTP_REFERER
entries in HTTP requests) and then used to imperson-
ate that specific user. This is hard to battle, but one
convenient way to make it harder for attackers is to
change the session ID whenever something "important" happens, such as the user signing in. For instance,
Amazon requires users who are already authenticated
with their cookie to sign in again when they want to
order something.

In this case, the function session_regenerate_id() just
changes the current session ID but leaves all data intact.
This is shown in the preceding code, in which the current session ID (both old and new) is retrieved using
the session_id() function. Figure 6.7 shows a possible
output of this script.

NOTE: This code uses output buffering—
ob_start() and ob_end_flush()—because
session_regenerate_id() must also be called
before any HTML output is sent to the client.

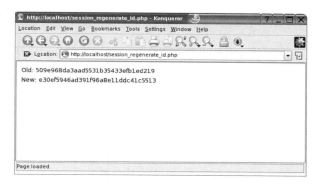

Figure 6.7   Two session IDs (one old, one new)

Implementing a Custom Session Management

```
session_set_save_handler(
  'sess_open', 'sess_close', 'sess_read',
  'sess_write', 'sess_destroy', 'sess_gc');
```

A Custom Session Management (session_mysqli.inc.php; excerpt)

There are some good reasons not to store session data in files. Performance might be one issue, with security as another issue. An alternative way to store session information is to use databases. For this, you just need a database table called sessiondata with three columns. The names might vary, but the following ones are used in the upcoming code listings in this phrase:

- Column id (primary key) is of type VARCHAR(32) and contains the session ID.

- Column `data` is of type `TEXT` and contains the session data.
- Column `access` is of type `VARCHAR(14)` and contains the time stamp of the most recent access to the session information.

It doesn't matter which database is used. This phrase uses MySQL and PHP5's new `mysqli` extension, but it is easy to change the code to work with other databases, as well. (See Chapter 8, "Working with MySQL Databases," and Chapter 9, "Working with Other Databases," for information about using many relevant databases with PHP.)

You can use the PHP function `session_set_save_handler()`to provide custom functions for all relevant six session operations PHP uses internally:

- Opening a session
- Closing a session
- Reading a session variable
- Writing a session variable
- Destroying a session
- Cleaning up (garbage collection [for example, removing old session data from the data store])

For all six of these operations, the following listing contains code that reads and writes session data from and to a MySQL data source. You just need PHP 5 and have to set the connection parameters (server, username, password) appropriately. Then, you include the code from this listing using `require_once` and then use sessions as usual. In the background, PHP then saves all session information in the database and not in the file system:

```php
<?php
  $GLOBALS['sess_server'] = 'localhost';
  $GLOBALS['sess_db'] = 'sessions';
  $GLOBALS['sess_username'] = 'user';
  $GLOBALS['sess_password'] = 'pass';

  function sess_open() {
    $GLOBALS['sess_mysqli'] = mysqli_connect(
      $GLOBALS['sess_server'],
      $GLOBALS['sess_username'],
      $GLOBALS['sess_password']
    );
    mysqli_select_db($GLOBALS['sess_mysqli'],
➥$GLOBALS['sess_db']);
  }

  function sess_close() {
    mysqli_close($GLOBALS['sess_mysqli']);
  }

  function sess_read($id) {
    $result = mysqli_query(
      $GLOBALS['sess_mysqli'],
      sprintf('SELECT data FROM sessiondata WHERE id
➥= \'%s\'',
        mysqli_real_escape_string($GLOBALS
➥['sess_mysqli'], $id))
    );
    if ($row = mysqli_fetch_object($result)) {
      $ret = $row->data;
      mysqli_query(
        $GLOBALS['sess_mysqli'],
        sprintf('UPDATE sessiondata SET
➥access=\'%s\' WHERE id=\'\'',
          date('YmdHis'),
```

```
          mysqli_real_escape_string($GLOBALS
➥['sess_mysqli'], $id))
      );
    } else {
      $ret = '';
    }
    return $ret;
  }

  function sess_write($id, $data) {
    mysqli_query(
      $GLOBALS['sess_mysqli'],
      sprintf('UPDATE sessiondata SET data=\'%s\',
➥access=\'%s\' WHERE id=\'%s\'',
        mysqli_real_escape_string($GLOBALS
['sess_mysqli'], $data),
        date('YmdHis'),
        mysqli_real_escape_string($GLOBALS
➥['sess_mysqli'], $id))
    );
    if
➥(mysqli_affected_rows($GLOBALS['sess_mysqli']) < 1)
➥{
      mysqli_query(
        $GLOBALS['sess_mysqli'],
        sprintf('INSERT INTO sessiondata (data,
➥access, id) VALUES (\'%s\', \'%s\', \'%s\')',
          mysqli_real_escape_string($GLOBALS
['sess_mysqli'], $data),
          date('YmdHis'),
          mysqli_real_escape_string($GLOBALS
➥['sess_mysqli'], $id))
```

```
      );
    }
    return true;
  }

  function sess_destroy($id) {
    mysqli_query(
      $GLOBALS['sess_mysqli'],
      sprintf('DELETE FROM sessiondata WHERE
➥id=\'%s\'',
        mysqli_real_escape_string($GLOBALS
➥['sess_mysqli'], $id))
    );
    return true;
  }

  function sess_gc($timeout) {
    $timestamp = date('YmdHis', time() - $timeout);
    mysqli_query(
      $GLOBALS['sess_mysqli'],
      sprintf('DELETE FROM sessiondata WHERE access
➥< \'%s\'',
        $timestamp)
    );
  }

  session_set_save_handler(
    'sess_open', 'sess_close', 'sess_read',
    'sess_write', 'sess_destroy', 'sess_gc');
?>
```

A Custom Session Management (session_mysqli.inc.php)

NOTE: Starting with PHP 5.3 you can also use inline anonymous functions to set up the six save handler functions, as follows:

```
session_set_save_handler(
  function () { /* ... */ },
  function () { /* ... */ },
  function ($id) { /* ... */ },
  function ($id, $data) { /* ... */ },
  function ($id) { /* ... */ },
  function ($timeout) { /* ... */ });
```

TIP: The file session.sql in the download archive contains a SQL file to create the database table in MySQL. The file session_mysqli_readwrite.php uses the code in the preceding listing and saves some data in the session.

Figure 6.8 shows the contents in the session table after data has been written into it.

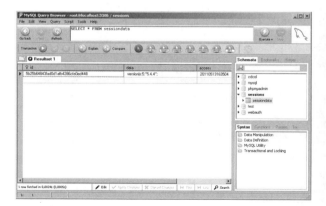

Figure 6.8   The session data now resides in the database.

Creating a Secured Area with Sessions

```
session_start();
if (!(isset($_SESSION['authorized']) &&
  $_SESSION['authorized'] != '')) {
  header("Location:
➥login.php?url={$_SERVER['PHP_SELF']}");
}
```

*Checking Whether the User Is Authenticated
(session_authentication.inc.php)*

Sessions can be a great way to secure certain parts of a Web site. The approach is simple: After the user is authenticated, write this information into a session variable. On all protected pages, check for the presence of this session variable.

You can first check for the session variable. The code from the beginning of this phrase must be included (with require_once) in all pages that are only accessible for authorized users.

The script login.php, to which the preceding code redirects the user, contains an HTML form (see also Figure 6.9) and checks whether the provided data is correct; you might have to add your own users and passwords, and also want to use encryption. As you might have seen, the previous URL is provided as a GET parameter. So, if available, the login code redirects users back to where they came from:

```php
<?php
  if (isset($_POST['user']) && $_POST['user'] ==
➥'Damon' &&
      isset($_POST['pass']) && $_POST['pass'] ==
➥'secret') {
    session_start();
    $_SESSION['authorized'] = 'ok';
    $url = (isset($_GET['url'])) ? $_GET['url'] :
➥'index.php';
    header("Location: $url");
  }
?>
```

Checking User Credentials (login.php; excerpt)

And that's it! The script secret.php in the download archive contains some quite secret information and is protected by the code in the two preceding listings.

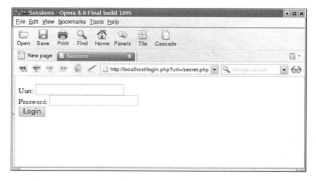

Figure 6.9   The login form. Note the referring page in the URL.

Creating a Secured Area without Sessions

```
$_SERVER['PHP_AUTH_USER'] == 'Shelley' &&
    $_SERVER['PHP_AUTH_PW'] == 'TopSecret'
```

```php
<?php
if (!(isset($_SERVER['PHP_AUTH_USER']) &&
    isset($_SERVER['PHP_AUTH_PW']) &&
    $_SERVER['PHP_AUTH_USER'] == 'Shelley' &&
    $_SERVER['PHP_AUTH_PW'] == 'TopSecret')) {
  header('WWW-Authenticate: Basic realm="Secured
➥area"');
  header('Status: 401 Unauthorized');
} else {
?>
<!DOCTYPE html PUBLIC "-//W3C//DTD XHTML 1.0
➥Transitional//EN" "http://www.w3.org/TR/xhtml1/DTD/
➥xhtml1-transitional.dtd">
...
<?php
}
?>
```

Using HTTP to Secure PHP Pages (http_authentication.php; excerpt)

If using authentication with PHP's session management seems to be too much overhead, you have two other options:

- Configure your Web server so that only authorized users can access some files or directories. For instance, Apache users might use .htaccess files; http://httpd.apache.org/docs/current/howto/htaccess.html contains some good information about that. Microsoft IIS offers a graphical user interface (GUI) administration of access rights, so that can be done, as well.

- A more-or-less platform-independent way to secure your Web site is to use authentication via HTTP. If you send an HTTP status code 401 (unauthorized), browsers prompt the client for a username and a password. This information is then available using $_SERVER['PHP_AUTH_USER'] and $_SERVER['PHP_AUTH_PW']—however, only if you are running PHP as a server module, not in Common Gateway Interface (CGI) mode.

You can then check this and decide whether to send out a 401 header again or to show the page's actual contents. The preceding listing shows an implementation for that. Figure 6.10 shows the prompt for a username and password.

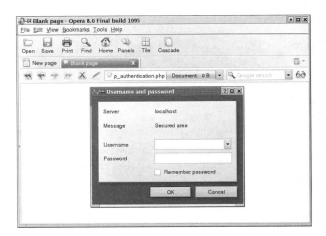

Figure 6.10   The browser prompts for a username and a password.

What Does PEAR Offer?

The following PHP Extension and Application Repository (PEAR) packages offer functionality that can be associated to sessions and HTTP authentication:

- Auth implements various ways to authenticate users and, therefore, protect PHP pages.
- HTTP_Session is based upon PHP's session mechanism but offers an object-oriented access to session information.

7

Using Files on the Server File System

Although databases are very common, using the file system to store data can be a real alternative. Often, it is easier to implement that way. Sometimes, it is faster, and much more important, all hosting providers have file access enabled, whereas database support might only be available at extra cost.

PHP supports working with files through a set of certain functions. Using wrappers, the same technologies can also be used to access remote data via protocols such as Hypertext Transfer Protocol (HTTP) or File Transfer Protocol (FTP), but this is covered in more detail in Chapter 9, "Communicating with Others."

This chapter covers both standard tasks such as reading and writing files, and advanced tasks such as archiving files in ZIP or BZ2 format. Many of these tasks can be solved in different, equally usable ways, so you truly have the freedom of choice.

Opening and Closing Files

```
$fp = @fopen('file.txt', 'at');
fclose($fp);
```

```php
<?php
  if ($fp = @fopen('file.txt', 'at')) {
    echo 'File opened.';
    fclose($fp);
    echo '<br />File closed.';
  } else {
    echo 'Error opening file.';
  }
?>
```

Opening (and Closing) Files (fopen.php)

For most file system functions, the files have to be opened first. The function fopen() does exactly this and returns a so-called file handle, a pointer to the file. This file handle can then be used in subsequent functions to, for instance, read information from a file or write to it.

fopen() expects at least two parameters:

- The name of the file
- The file mode to use when accessing the file

Of great interest is the file mode parameter. This is a string that consists of one or more characters. The first character is one of a, r, w, or x; after that, one or more special modifiers can be used. Table 7.1 shows all modes.

Table 7.1   **File Modes for PHP's File Functions**

Mode	Description
a	Open file to append (write) data; create it if it doesn't exist
a+	As mode a, but additionally with read access to the file
r	Open file to read data
r+	As mode r, but in addition with write access to the file
w	Open file to write data, erasing its contents; create it if it doesn't exist
w+	As mode w, but in addition with read access to the file
x	Create file to write data; send E_WARNING if it already exists
x+	As mode x, but in addition with read access to the file

So, the modifier + always adds the missing read or write access to a file mode. There are other modifiers, as well. PHP does a decent job determining whether a file is a text file or a binary file and translates funny characters appropriately. If you append b to a file mode, you force PHP to open a file as a binary file; for instance, the file mode rb opens a file for reading in binary mode.

Another special modifier exists that might come in handy for Windows users: t. If this is appended to the file mode, all \n line breaks are converted into \r\n as Windows applications might expect.

fopen() returns a file handle or false if opening the file did not work. You should, however, suppress any potential error messages with the @ character.

As soon as a file is not used anymore, it should be closed. PHP automatically closes all open files upon termination of the script; however, to use the system resources as efficiently as possible, files should be closed as early as possible to free up memory and speed up the system. For this, use `fclose()` and provide the file handle as a parameter.

The code at the beginning of this phrase uses both `fopen()` and `fclose()`.

After running the script, a file called `file.txt` is created.

NOTE: For this (and other examples in this chapter) to work, you have to make sure that the PHP script has the appropriate rights for the file to access. Usually, Apache runs either under a special user account like nobody, apache, www-data (UNIX/Linux) or under a regular user account (Windows). Use `chmod` to set the access privileges accordingly.

Microsoft IIS (Internet Information Services) runs PHP scripts under a special guest account called `IUSR_<name of machine>`. You can use the graphical user interface shown in Figure 7.1 to tune the access settings for files or directories.

TIP: To avoid any mistakes when trying to access non-existent files, you can use the function `file_exists()`, which returns regardless of whether a given filename exists.

```
if (file_exists('file.txt'), 'r') {
  // ...
}
```

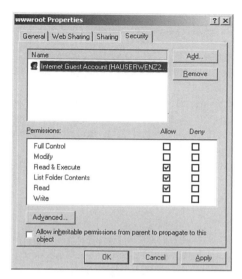

Figure 7.1   Allowing the IIS user to access a file or directory

Reading from Files

```
echo file_get_contents('file.txt');
```

To read data from a file, PHP offers several possibilities. Probably the easiest way is to read it all at once and then output it to the user.

The function file_get_contents() returns the contents of a file (or stream) as a string so that it all can be processed further. The following code reads in a file called file.txt and prints out its contents. This function is binary safe, and that's why no file mode can (or has to) be used:

```php
<?php
  echo file_get_contents('file.txt');
?>
```

The file() function works as file_get_contents(), but returns the file's contents as an array: Each element is one row in the file (including the line break character). The following code converts this array into a string and sends it to the browser. The function implode() glues the array element together; see Chapter 2, "Working with Arrays":

```php
<?php
  echo implode('', file('file.txt'));
?>
```

For maximum flexibility, the manual way can be used; however, for text files, this is often not needed. Open the file with fopen(), and then call fgets() as long as data is returned (a while loop is convenient here) and output the data. fgets() returns as many characters as are provided in its second parameter but, at most, all characters until the end of the current line:

```php
<?php
  $fp = fopen('file.txt', 'r');
  while (!feof($fp)) {
    $line = fgets($handle, 4096);
    echo $line;
  }
  fclose($fp);
?>
```

Sending a File's Contents to the Browser, Line by Line (readfile-linebyline.php)

Writing to Files

```
file_put_contents('file.txt', "--> This text file
contains\nsome random text. <--");
```

```php
<?php
  file_put_contents('file.txt',
    "--> This text file contains\nsome random text.
<--");
  echo 'File written.';
?>
```

Writing Data into a File (file_put_contents.php)

Writing to files is as easy as reading from them—if you are using PHP 5 or later. Then, the function file_put_contents() writes data directly to a file, and this is binary safe. After calling the function, the file is closed. The preceding code writes data into a file.

However, the preceding code overwrites the existing file. If you want to append data (therefore emulating file mode a), you first have to read in the file's data:

```php
<?php
  function file_append_contents($filename, $data) {
    $olddata = @file_get_contents($filename);
    return file_put_contents($filename,
"$olddata$data");
  }

  file_append_contents('file.txt',
    "\n--> This text file contains\neven more random
text. <--");
  echo 'Data appended to file';
?>
```

Appending Data to a File (file_append_contents.php)

TIP: It is even easier to provide a third parameter to file_put_contents() to append data instead of overwriting files:

```
file_put_contents($filename, $data, FILE_APPEND);
```

Locking Files

```
flock($fp, LOCK_EX);
```

```php
<?php
  if (!function_exists('file_put_contents')) {
    function file_put_contents($filename, $content)
➡{
      if ($fp = @fopen($filename, 'w') && flock($fp,
➡LOCK_EX)) {
        $result = fwrite($fp, $content);
        flock($fp, LOCK_UN);
        fclose($fp);
        return $result;
      } else {
        return false;
      }
    }
  }
?>
```

Using file_put_contents() with a File Lock (flock.php; excerpts)

While reading and writing files, you have to take concurrency into mind. What if two processes try to access the file at the same time? To avoid trouble when one process writes while the other one reads, you have to lock the file. This is done using the PHP function flock().

The first parameter is the file handle; the second one is the desired kind of locking to be used. The following options are available:

- **LOCK_EX**—Exclusive lock for writing
- **LOCK_NB**—Nonblocking lock
- **LOCK_SH**—Shared lock for reading
- **LOCK_UN**—Releasing a lock

The preceding code contains an updated version of the custom `file_put_contents()` function from the previous phrase, this time using an exclusive lock.

Using Relative Paths for File Access

```
dirname(__FILE__)
basename(__FILE__)
```

```php
<?php
  $directory = dirname(__FILE__);
  $filename = basename(__FILE__);
  print "This script is called $filename and resides
➡in $directory.";
?>
```

Determining Directory Name and Filename (pathinfos.php)

Usually, files are opened (or searched) relative to the path of the document. If you are using PHP as an ISAPI module under Windows, the location of `php5.dll` or `php5ts.dll` may be relevant. To be sure that you are searching to the current scripts' path, you can use a two-step approach:

- The constant __FILE__ contains the full path of the current script.

- The function dirname() determines the directory name portion of a path.

To use a relative path, you can now call dirname(__FILE__) and then attach the relative path, taking into consideration the directory separator character, which is / on UNIX/Linux, \ on Windows, and : on Mac OS X. PHP tells you the system´s default in its DIRECTORY_SEPARATOR constant.

The sister function to dirname() is basename(); this one determines the filename portion of a path.

The listing at the beginning of this phrase uses both basename() and dirname() and __FILE__ to determine information about the current path: directory and filename. Figure 7.2 shows the script's output.

Figure 7.2   Detecting the script's name and its directory

Avoiding Security Traps with File Access

One very important point: If you are using files with PHP, avoid retrieving the filename from external sources, such as user input or cookies. This might allow users to inject dangerous code in your Web site or force you to load files you did not want to open. Some so-called security experts had a self-programmed content management system that created uniform resource locators (URLs) like this: `index.php?page=subpage.html`. This just loaded the page `subpage.html` into some kind of page template and sent this to the browser. But what if the following URL is called: `index.php?page=../../../etc/passwd`? With some luck (or bad luck, depending on your point of view), the contents of the file `/etc/passwd` are printed out in the browser. This kind of attack—a so-called directory traversal attack—is quite common on the Web. However, you can avoid becoming a victim in several ways:

- If possible, do not use dynamic data in filenames.

- If you have to use dynamic data in filenames, use `basename()` to determine the actual name of the file, omitting the path information, and verify and validate the user input as extensively as possible.

- Set the `php.ini` directive `open_basedir`. This expects a list of directories where PHP may access files. PHP checks the basedir rules whenever a file is opened, and refuses to do so if it isn't in the appropriate path. However, this is not a foolproof mechanism (for instance, it works only for PHP files) and can never be the only defense against attack, just one piece of the puzzle.

- Set `include_path` to a directory you put all to-be-used files into and set the third parameter to `fopen()` to `true`, using the `include_path`.

Working with CSV Data

`fgetcsv($fp, 4096)`

```php
<table>
<?php
  $fp = fopen('file.csv', 'r');
  while (!feof($fp)) {
    $line = fgetcsv($fp, 4096);
    echo '<tr><td>';
    echo implode('</td><td>',
➥htmlspecialchars($line));
    echo '</td></tr>';
  }
  fclose($fp);
?>
</table>
```

Reading CSV Information (fgetcsv.php)

CSV is a file format and stands for comma-separated values. Many spreadsheet applications can export their data into CSV files. It seems to be easy to use explode() to convert CSV values into arrays; however, this turns out to be really complicated. What if there is a comma within a value? Then, the content is surrounded by double quotes, which makes it hard to use explode().

As (almost) always, the PHP project has done most of the work and offers fgetcsv(). This function works as fgets(); however, it converts the line into an array, separating the contents at a comma (or any other character provided in the third parameter).

The second parameter to fgetcsv() is the maximum length of a line in the CSV file. This is optional in PHP 5. So you need to check the length of the longest line in the CSV file; otherwise, data will get truncated.

The code at the beginning of this phrase reads in a CSV file and outputs it as an HTML table. This is done using the following code within a loop:

```
$line = fgetcsv($handle, 4096);
echo '<tr><td>';
echo implode('</td><td>', $line);
echo '</td></tr>';
```

This creates a row in an HTML table:
<tr><td>...</td></tr>.

Figure 7.3 shows both the original spreadsheet file (in OpenOffice.org) and the result in the browser.

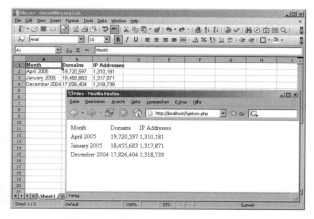

Figure 7.3 The CSV spreadsheet in OpenOffice.org and the result in the browser (fgetcsv.php; excerpt)

NOTE: In the code at the beginning of this phrase, the output is not sanitized using htmlspecialchars()—in this case, to make the code short. However, depending on the data you have, you should consider running htmlspecialchars() on all elements of the array's fgetcsv() returns.

For writing PHP files, PHP offers a sister function, fputcsv().You provide a file pointer and an array of values, and PHP does the rest, including escaping special characters. This function was introduced in PHP 5.1. Basically, you just join all array elements with commas.You also have to take care of commas within the elements, so you surround all values by double quotes. If the element contains double quotes, these have to be escaped. However, this is not done using backslashes, but by doubling the quotes. The following is an example for a valid line of CSV data:

```
Quote,"And she said: ""No."" ...",Unknown
```

The following is the code for fputcsv() for older PHP versions:

```
if (!function_exists('fputcsv')) {
  function fputcsv($fp, $line, $separator = ',') {
    for ($i=0; $i < count($line); $i++) {
      if (false !== strpos($line[$i], '"')) {
        $line[$i] = ereg_replace('"', '""',
$line[$i]);
      }
      if (false !== strpos($line[$i], $separator) ||
          false !== strpos($line[$i], '"')) {
        $line[$i] = '"' . $line[$i] . '"';
      }
    }
    fwrite($fp, implode($separator, $line) .
➥"\r\n");
```

```
    }
  }
```

The following code uses the fputcsv() function to manually create the CSV file that was used previously:

```php
<?php
  // ...

  $data = array(
    array('April 2005', '19,720,597', '1,310,181'),
    array('January 2005', '18,455,683',
➥'1,317,871'),
    array('December 2004', '17,826,404',
➥'1,318,739')
  );

  if ($fp = @fopen('usage.csv', 'w')) {
    foreach ($data as $line) {
      fputcsv($fp, $line);
    }
    fclose($fp);
    echo 'CSV written.';
  } else {
    echo 'Cannot open file.';
  }
?>
```

Writing CSV Information (fputcsv.php; excerpt)

This code creates the file usage.csv with the following contents:

```
April 2005,"19,720,597","1,310,181"
January 2005,"18,455,683","1,317,871"
December 2004,"17,826,404","1,318,739"
```

Parsing INI Files

```
parse_ini_file('php.ini', true);
```

```php
<?php
  echo '<xmp>' .
    print_r(parse_ini_file('php.ini', true), true) .
    '</xmp>';
?>
```

Reading Information from INI Files (parse_ini_file.php)

Another file format that is very well known is the INI
file format. It was very widely used in the Windows
world, but today also drives the configuration of complex software products like PHP. For instance, take a
look at php.ini. Here is a (modified) excerpt from the
default php.ini that shows very well the structure of
INI files:

```
[mail function]
; For Win32 only.
; SMTP = localhost
; For Unix only.  You may supply arguments as well
➡(default: "sendmail -t -i").
sendmail_path =
```

So, there are sections that start with a section headline
in square brackets, comments that start with a semi-
colon, and settings in the format name=value. The PHP
function parse_ini_file() now reads in such a PHP
file and creates an array out of it: Each section is a
subarray, and within those subarrays you find the
names and the values of directives in the INI file. The
code at the beginning of this phrase does this (remember to change the path to php.ini, if appropriate), and
Figure 7.4 shows the output.

Figure 7.4 The contents of php.ini as a multidimensional array (parse_ini_file.php; excerpt).

TIP: If you want to avoid the grouping by sections in the INI file, just omit the second parameter parse_ini_file(); then, you get all settings at once.

```
parse_ini_file('php.ini');
```

Retrieving File Information

```
$filename = __FILE__;
```

```php
<?php
  $filename = __FILE__;
  $data = array(
    'fileatime' => fileatime($filename),
    'filegroup' => filegroup($filename),
```

```
   'filemtime' => filemtime($filename),
   'fileowner' => fileowner($filename),
   'filesize' => filesize($filename),
   'is_dir' => var_export(is_dir($filename), true),
   'is_executable' =>
➥var_export(is_executable($filename), true),
   'is_file' => var_export(is_file($filename),
➥true),
   'is_link' => var_export(is_link($filename),
➥true),
   'is_readable' => var_export(is_readable
➥($filename), true),
   'is_uploaded_file' =>
➥var_export(is_uploaded_file($filename), true),
   'is_writable' => var_export(is_writable
➥($filename), true)
 );

 echo '<table>';
 foreach ($data as $function => $result) {
   echo
➥"<tr><td>$function</td><td>$result</td></tr>";
 }
 echo '</table>';
?>
```

Reading Information about Files (fileinfos.php)

It is rather unusual to use PHP for accessing directory and file information—at least as long as the vast majority of PHP scripts run via HTTP in a Web server and not using the command-line interface (CLI) or PHP. However, PHP offers a variety of helper functions that provide information about a file. Most of them are just calling the relevant operating system functions.

The following list shows the most relevant helper functions in this regard:

- `fileatime($filename)`—Last access to the file
- `filegroup($filename)`—Group that owns the file
- `filemtime($filename)`—Last change to the file
- `fileowner($filename)`—File owner
- `filesize($filename)`—Size of the file

Another set of helper functions also takes a filename, which means that the files do not have to be opened before you use these functions:

- `is_dir($path)`—Whether the path is a directory
- `is_executable($filename)`—Whether the filename is an executable
- `is_file($path)`—Whether the path is a (regular) file
- `is_link($filename)`—Whether the filename is a symbolic link
- `is_readable($filename)`—Whether the file is readable
- `is_uploaded_file($path)`—Whether the path is a file uploaded via HTTP (see Chapter 5, "Remembering Users (Cookies and Sessions)")
- `is_writable($filename)`—Whether the file is writable

Figure 7.5 contains the result of the code at the beginning of this phrase.

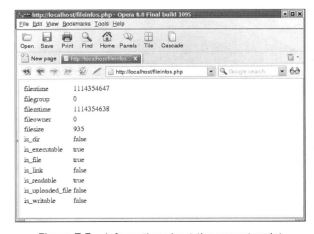

Figure 7.5   Information about the current script
(fileinfos.php)

Copying, Moving, and Deleting Files

```
copy($filename, $tempname1);
rename($tempname1, $tempname2);
unlink($tempname2);
```

```php
<?php
  $filename = 'php.ini';
  $tempname1 = $filename . rand();
  $tempname2 = $filename . rand();
  copy($filename, $tempname1);
  echo "Copied to $tempname1<br />";
  rename($tempname1, $tempname2);
  echo "Moved to $tempname2<br />";
  unlink($tempname2);
  echo "File deleted.";
?>
```

Copying, Moving, and Deleting Files (copymovedelete.php)

Many other standard command-line functions of many operating systems are available in PHP. This not only includes chmod() and chgrp(), but also the following file system operations:

- **copy()**—Copies a file
- **rename()**—Moves a file
- **unlink()**—Deletes a file

The preceding code duplicates the current file, moves it (or renames it), and finally deletes the resulting file.

Browsing the File System

```
$d = dir('.');
while (false !== ($file = $d->read()))
```

```php
<?php
  $d = dir('.');
  while (false !== ($file = $d->read())) {
    echo htmlspecialchars($file) . '<br />';
  }
  $d->close();
?>
```

Reading a Directory's Contents with PHP's dir *Class (dir.php)*

Since the ancient PHP 3 (!), PHP comes with a built-in class. This sounds strange because OOP (object-oriented programming) did not become "mainstream" in PHP before version 5; however, this special class offers several methods to access the file system. It is possible to get a list of all entries in a directory.

You instantiate the class without the keyword new, just by providing the desired path as a parameter. Then the method read() iterates through the list of entries. The preceding code does exactly this and prints out the contents of the current directory.

Note that the two directory entries . (current directory) and .. (parent directory, if you are not in the root directory) are printed out.

Using PHP Streams

```php
<?php
  $filename = __FILE__;
  $zipfile = "$filename.zip";

  $data = file_get_contents(__FILE__);
  echo 'Loaded file (size: ' . strlen($data) .
➥').<br />';

  file_put_contents("compress.zlib://$zipfile",
➥$data);
  echo 'Zipped file (new size: ' .
➥filesize($zipfile) . ').<br />';

  $data = file_get_contents("compress.zlib:
➥//$zipfile");
  echo 'Original file size: ' . strlen($data) . '.';
?>
```

Zipping and Unzipping a File (zip.php; excerpt)

In PHP, the concept of PHP streams was introduced. Since then, there is a common denominator for all kinds of resources: files, HTTP and FTP data, and even archive file formats. You can find greater detail about the networking aspect of this in Chapter 11, "Communicating with Others", this chapter just picks out some file-specific features: compression streams.

One of them can be used to use ZIP files. The pseudo protocol `compress.zlib://` can be used to access ZIP files as you would access regular files. For this to work, you have to use the configuration switch `-with-gzip` under UNIX/Linux; Windows systems have the required libraries already included. Then, you can use the files using—for instance, `file_get_contents()` and `file_put_contents()`.

The preceding code loads the current file (with `file_get_contents()`), zips it, and writes it to the hard disk (with `file_put_contents()`). Then, it reads in the zipped file (with `file_get_contents()`) and compares the file sizes.

When testing this, the code managed to compress the file from 729 bytes to 336 bytes.

Alternatively, you can use PHP's built-in ZIP functions, which are implemented by a wrapper to the ZZIPlib library from http://zziplib.sourceforge.net/. This one can only read data from a ZIP file, unfortunately, but also supports multiple files within an archive (when using the stream wrapper `compress.zlib://`, you first have to tar data to support multiple files).

To install, use `extension=php_zip.dll` in `php.ini` under Windows, or configure PHP with `-with-zip`, providing the path to ZZIPlib. The following steps must be taken to use this extension:

1. Open the archive using `zip_open()`.

2. Iterate through the archive's entries with `zip_read()`.

3. Read a specific file using `zip_entry_open()` and `zip_entry_read()`.

The following code shows the contents of a ZIP archive and determines the names and file size of all entries:

```php
<?php
  $zipfile = dirname(__FILE__) . '/archive.zip';
  if ($zip = zip_open($zipfile)) {
    while ($file = zip_read($zip)) {
      printf('%s (%d)<br />',
        zip_entry_name($file),
➥zip_entry_filesize($file)
      );
    }
    zip_close($zip);
  }
?>
```

Unzipping a File Using ZZIPlib (zziplib.php)

Using Bzip2 Archives

```php
file_put_contents("compress.bzip2://$bzip2file",
$data);
```

```php
<?php
  $filename = __FILE__;
  $bzip2file = "$filename.bz2";

  $data = file_get_contents(__FILE__);
  echo 'Loaded file (size: ' . strlen($data) . '
➥).<br />';

  file_put_contents("compress.bzip2://$bzip2file",
➥$data);
  echo 'Bzipped file (new size: ' .
➥filesize($bzip2file) . ').<br />';
```

```
  $data =
➥file_get_contents("compress.bzip2://$bzip2file");
  echo 'Original file size: ' . strlen($data) . '.';
?>
```

Zipping and Unzipping a File with Bzip2 (bzip2.php; excerpt)

Another file format that does not come with all operating systems, but which offers great compression rates, is Bzip2. Here, PHP also has a built-in stream wrapper: compress.bzip2://. To use this, you have to load the Bzip2 library from http://sources.redhat.com/bzip2/. Then use the configuration switch –with-bzip2 (UNIX/Linux), or write extension=php_bzip2.dll in your php.ini configuration file (Windows). Then you are ready to go and can compress or decompress files, as shown in the preceding code, which uses file_get_contents() and file_put_contents().

Alternatively, you can use PHP's special Bzip2 functions. They work very similarly to PHP's file functions. However, for writing, you have to use bzopen(), bzwrite(), and bzclose() instead of fopen(), fwrite(), and fclose(), as the following code shows, which creates a function file_put_bzip2_contents():

```php
<?php
  function file_put_bzip2_contents($filename,
➥$content) {
    if ($fp = @bzopen($filename, 'wb')) {
      $result = bzwrite($fp, $content);
      bzclose($fp);
      return $result;
    } else {
      return false;
    }
```

```
  }
  file_put_bzip2_contents('file.txt.bz2',
    "\n--> This text file contains\nsome random
➡text. <--");
  echo 'Data written to file.';
?>
```

Zipping a File with Bzip2 (bzip2write.php)

The other direction (reading a file from a BZip2
archive) works analogously to reading a regular file.
Instead of fopen(), fread(), and fclose(), you use
bzopen(), bzread(), and bclose(), as shown in the
following code, which writes a function
file_get_bzip2_contents():

```php
<?php
  function file_get_bzip2_contents($filename) {
    $result = '';
    if ($fp = @bzopen($filename, 'wb')) {
      while ($data = bzread($fp, 4096)) {
        $result .= $data;
      }
      bzclose($fp);
      return $result;
    } else {
      return false;
    }
  }

  echo nl2br(htmlspecialchars(
    file_get_bzip2_contents('file.txt.bz2')
  ));
?>
```

Unzipping a File with Bzip2 (bzip2read.php)

Returning Files with an HTTP Request

```
$filename = 'httpfile.zip';
header("Content-Disposition: attachment; filename =
➥$filename");
```

```php
<?php
  $filename = 'httpfile.zip';
  $mimetype = 'application/zip';
  $data = file_get_contents($filename);
  $size = strlen($data);

  header("Content-Disposition: attachment; filename
➥= $filename");
  header("Content-Length: $size");
  header("Content-Type: $mimetype");
  echo $data;
?>
```

Sending a File with HTTP (httpfile.php)

When a PHP script shall return a (downloadable) file instead of HTML, the correct HTTP headers have to be sent:

- `Content-Disposition` for the (proposed) name of the file

- `Content-Length` for the file size

- `Content-Type` for the MIME type of the file

The preceding code reads in a ZIP file and sends it to the client; Figure 7.6 shows its result in the browser.

Figure 7.6   The browser wants to save the file.

What Does PEAR Offer?

The following PHP Extension and Application Repository (PEAR) packages offer functionality that can be used for working with files and streams:

- `File` offers some helper functions for file access, some of them deprecated to new functionality in more recent PHP releases.
- `File_Find` searches a path for certain files or patterns.
- `File_SearchReplace` does a Search and Replace within files.
- `Stream_Var` allows you to save variables in streams so that you can access them like you would access files or streams.

8

Working with MySQL Databases

One of the main strengths of PHP is its support for a vast number of databases. Very often, PHP and MySQL are viewed as an entity. However, other databases have their strengths, too. For instance, it took MySQL quite some time to support features that are considered standard in other systems; however, MySQL is known to be very fast.

This chapter focuses on MySQL, whereas Chapter 9, "Working with Other Databases," tackles quite a number of other databases. Both chapters show the basic operations with them: connecting, sending SQL statements, and evaluating the return values. No matter what your database-driven web application must do, it always has to do these steps.

To have some test data, we created a database called phrasebook in the relational database management system (RDBMS) and put a table called quotes in there. This table consists of four fields:

- **id**—An integer value that is increased by one for each new entry entered into the database. Depending on the database system, the data type is either called IDENTITY, auto_increment, or something similar.

- **quote**—The quote, as a VARCHAR(255); this length works with all systems.

- **author**—The person who produced the quote, as a VARCHAR(50).

- **year**—The year the quote has been produced (sometimes, this is highly speculative), of type INT.

Every database system comes with either management tools or third-party products available. For instance, the PHP- based phpMyAdmin (http://www.phpmyadmin.net/) shown in Figure 8.1 offers very good access to a MySQL installation.

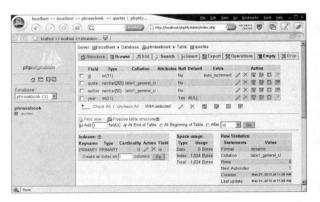

Figure 8.1   Managing a MySQL installation using phpMyAdmin

Connecting to MySQLi

```
@mysqli_connect('localhost', 'user', 'password')
```

```php
<?php
  if ($db = @mysqli_connect('localhost', 'user',
➥'password')) {
    mysqli_select_db($db, 'phrasebook');
    echo 'Connected to the database.';
    mysqli_close($db);
  } else {
    echo 'Connection failed.';
  }
?>
```

Connecting to MySQLi (mysqli_connect.php)

Several MySQL extensions for PHP are available. The oldest one, ext/mysql, was used for PHP 4 and older versions; its successor, ext/mysqli (the i officially stands for improved, and unofficially for incompatible—but that's cynical), comes with PHP 5 but requires MySQL 4.1 or later. However, PHP 5 also supports the old extension. Only the latter extension is covered in this chapter. A third option, PDO, is covered at the end of Chapter 9 because you can use this API with other databases, as well.

Apart from the different APIs, PHP users also have the option to choose between different libraries. Older PHP installations usually use the MySQL client server library (libmysql), but PHP 5.3 introduced the MySQL native driver (mysqlnd). This driver provides additional features and better performance, so it is recommended to use this driver.

If you want to use `ext/mysqli`, the switch for –with-mysql has to point to /path/to/mysql_config. Windows users have to use the files `php_mysqli.dll` and `lib-mysqli.dll`; the rest of the previous install instructions remain unchanged.

Now connecting to the database is easy: Just call `mysql_connect()`, providing the server, username, and password. You then get a handle that can be used for `mysqli_select_db()` or to choose a database on the server. Finally, `mysqli_close()` closes the connection to the data source.

If you have worked with the older `ext/mysql`, keep in mind that the different variable order for `mysql(i)_select_db()` is one of the prominent differences between the two extensions. The newer one wants the database handle first. Another difference between these two extensions is that the database handle is a mandatory parameter whenever used. With `ext/mysql`, the last handle created by `mysql_connect()` is the current default handle for the page. One more difference: `mysqli_connect()` accepts the name of the database as an optional fourth parameter, so you can avoid using `mysqli_select_db()`.

NOTE: Alternatively, the `mysqli` extension also offers an object-oriented syntax to access a data source. Although this chapter uses the functional approach to make a possible transition from `ext/mysql` to `ext/mysqli` as painless as possible, the following shows what the object-oriented approach looks like:

```
$db = new mysqli('localhost', 'user',
➥'password');
$db->select_db('phrasebook');
$db->close();
```

Sending SQL to MySQL

`mysqli_query()`

```php
<?php
  if ($db = @mysqli_connect('localhost', 'user',
➡'password')) {
    require_once 'stripFormSlashes.inc.php';
    mysqli_select_db($db, 'phrasebook');
    mysqli_query($db, sprintf(
      'INSERT INTO quotes (quote, author, year)
➡VALUES (\'%s\', \'%s\', \'%s\')',
      mysqli_real_escape_string($db,
➡$_POST['quote']),
      mysqli_real_escape_string($db,
➡$_POST['author']),
      intval($_POST['year'])));
    echo 'Quote saved.';
    mysqli_close($db);
  } else {
    echo 'Connection failed.';
  }
?>
```

Sending SQL to MySQLi (mysqli_query.php; excerpt)

The function `mysqli_query()` sends SQL to a database
identified by a handle—second parameter for
`mysql_query()`, first parameter for `mysqli_query()`.
However, to avoid an attack called SQL injection (a
method to inject SQL statements using GET or POST
data), you absolutely *must* use
`mysqli_real_escape_string()`to escape any dangerous
characters such as single quotes. See the preceding and
the following listing for implementations. The code
missing from those listings (but, of course, it is included

in the code download) is basically an HTML form that accepts a quote, its author, and a year. Figure 8.2 shows the HTML input form for the quote collection:

```php
<?php
  if ($db = @mysqli_connect('localhost', 'user',
➥'password')) {
    mysqli_select_db($db, 'phrasebook');
    mysqli_query($db, sprintf(
      'INSERT INTO quotes (quote, author, year)
➥VALUES (\'%s\', \'%s\', \'%s\')',
      mysqli_real_escape_string($db,
➥$_POST['quote']),
      mysqli_real_escape_string($db,
➥$_POST['author']),
      intval($_POST['year'])));
    echo 'Quote saved.';
    mysqli_close($db);
  } else {
    echo 'Connection failed.';
  }
?>
```

Sending SQL to MySQL (mysqli_query.php; excerpt)

Figure 8.2 The HTML input form for adding quotes to the database

Prepared Statements with MySQL

```
$stmt = mysqli_prepare();
mysqli_stmt_execute($stmt);
```

```php
<?php
  if ($db = @mysqli_connect('localhost', 'user',
➥'password')) {
    mysqli_select_db($db, 'phrasebook');
    $stmt = mysqli_prepare($db, 'INSERT INTO quotes
➥(quote, author, year) VALUES (?, ?, ?)');
    $quote = mysqli_real_escape_string($db,
➥$_POST['quote']);
    $author = mysqli_real_escape_string($db,
➥$_POST['author']);
    $year = intval($_POST['year']);
    mysqli_stmt_bind_param($stmt, 'ssi', $quote,
➥$author, $year);
    if (mysqli_stmt_execute($stmt)) {
      echo 'Quote saved.';
    } else {
      echo 'Error writing quote.';
    }
    mysqli_close($db);
  } else {
    echo 'Connection failed.';
  }
?>
```

Using Prepared Statements with MySQL
(mysqli_stmt_execute.php; excerpt)

The new MySQL extension offers a way to both avoid SQL injection and to speed up SQL statements: so-called prepared statements. Within them, you provide placeholders for any dynamic data you are using in the SQL code. You then assign values to those placeholders. The MySQL extension then takes care of all the rest, including escaping of special characters.

So first, you prepare an SQL statement with `mysqli_prepare()`; as a placeholder character, you use a question mark:

```
$stmt = mysqli_prepare($db, 'INSERT INTO quotes
➥(quote, author, year) VALUES (?, ?, ?)');
```

Then, you bind values to each parameter. First, you provide the statement returned by `mysqli_prepare`, and then one-character codes for the values of all parameters (s for string, i for integer, d for double). Then, you provide a list of values. Because these values are used by reference, you have to provide variables, not raw values:

```
mysqli_stmt_bind_param($stmt, 'ssi', $quote,
➥$author, $year);
```

Finally, `mysqli_stmt_execute()` executes the prepared statement.

Retrieving Results of a Query to MySQL

```
$result = mysqli_query(handle, query);
mysqli_fetch_object($result);
```

```
<table>
<tr><th>#</th><th>Quote</th><th>Author</th><th>Year<
➥/th></tr>
<?php
  if ($db = @mysqli_connect('localhost', 'user',
➥'password')) {
```

```
    mysqli_select_db($db, 'phrasebook');
    $result = mysqli_query($db, 'SELECT * FROM
➥quotes');
    while ($row = mysqli_fetch_object($result)) {
      printf(
        '<tr><td>%s</td><td>%s</td><td>%s</td><td>%s
➥</td></tr>',
        htmlspecialchars($row->id),
        htmlspecialchars($row->quote),
        htmlspecialchars($row->author),
        htmlspecialchars($row->year)
      );
    }
    mysqli_close($db);
  } else {
    echo '<tr><td colspan="4">Connection
➥failed.</td></tr>';
  }
?>
</table>
```

Retrieving Data from MySQL (mysqli_fetch.php; excerpt)

The return value of mysqli_query() is a pointer to the actual resultset. It can be used to iterate through the complete list of entries returned by a SELECT statement. For this, these functions come in handy:

- mysqli_fetch_assoc() returns the current row in the resultset as an associative array (field names become keys) and then moves on to the next row.

- mysqli_fetch_object() returns the current row in the resultset as an object (field names become properties) and then moves on to the next row.

- `mysqli_fetch_row()` returns the current row in the resultset as a numeric array and then moves on to the next row.

There are other functions, as well; however, these three are the ones used most often. The following code uses `mysqli_fetch_assoc()`, whereas the preceding listing prints out the contents of the database table with `mysqli_fetch_object()`. The main idea is to use a `while` loop—all `mysqli_fetch_*` functions return `false` when no data is left in the resultset:

```
<table>
<tr><th>#</th><th>Quote</th><th>Author</th><th>Year
➥/th></tr>
<?php
  if ($db = @mysqli_connect('localhost', 'user',
➥'password')) {
    mysql_select_db($db, 'phrasebook');
    $result = mysqli_query($db, 'SELECT * FROM
➥quotes');
    while ($row = mysqli_fetch_assoc($result)) {
      printf(
        '<tr><td>%s</td><td>%s</td><td>%s</td><td>
➥%s</td></tr>',
        htmlspecialchars($row['id']),
        htmlspecialchars($row['quote']),
        htmlspecialchars($row['author']),
        htmlspecialchars($row['year'])
      );
    }
    mysqli_close($db);
  } else {
    echo '<tr><td colspan="4">Connection
➥failed.</td></tr>';
```

```
  }
?>
</table>
```

Retrieving Data from MySQL (mysqli_fetch.php; excerpt)

Figure 8.3 shows the contents of the database after some (political) quotes have been filled in. (Sorry, I am not from the United States; I took the first ones I could find.)

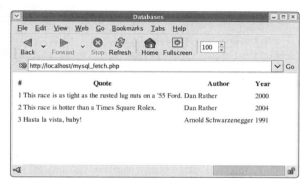

Figure 8.3   The contents of the database

Retrieving the Last Inserted ID

```
$id = mysqli_insert_id($db);
```

```php
<?php
  if ($db = @mysqli_connect('localhost', 'user',
➥'password')) {
    mysqli_select_db($db, 'phrasebook');
```

```
    mysqli_query($db, sprintf(
      'INSERT INTO quotes (quote, author, year)
➥VALUES (\'%s\', \'%s\', \'%s\')',
      mysqli_real_escape_string($db,
➥$_POST['quote']),
      mysqli_real_escape_string($db,
➥$_POST['author']),
      intval($_POST['year'])));
    $id = mysqli_insert_id($db);
    echo "Quote saved (ID=$id).';
    mysqli_close($db);
  } else {
    echo 'Connection failed.';
  }
?>
```

Retrieving the ID of the Previously Inserted Item with MySQL
(mysqli_insert_id.php; excerpt)

When using MySQL's `auto_increment` feature, the
database automatically assigns a value for that column
whenever you insert a new item into the table. It might
be interesting to determine this generated value after
the insert. The `mysqli_insert_id()` function can help us
here. Just provide the database connection handle, and
you will receive the ID in return. The value is only
available for the last INSERT SQL statement executed
with the provided connection.

Using Transactions

```
mysqli_autocommit($db, false);
mysqli_commit($db);
```

```php
<?php
  if ($db = @mysqli_connect('localhost', 'user',
➥'password')) {
    mysqli_select_db($db, 'phrasebook');
    mysqli_autocommit($db, false);
    if (mysqli_query($db, sprintf(
      'INSERT INTO quotes (quote, author, year)
➥VALUES (\'%s\', \'%s\', \'%s\')',
      mysqli_real_escape_string($db,
➥$_POST['quote']),
      mysqli_real_escape_string($db,
➥$_POST['author']),
      intval($_POST['year'])))) {
      $result = mysqli_query($db, 'SELECT MAX(id)
➥FROM quotes');
      $row = mysqli_fetch_object($result);
      $id = $row->id;
      mysqli_commit($db);
      echo "Quote saved (ID=$id).';
    } else {
      mysqli_rollback($db);
      echo 'An error has occurred.';
    }
    mysqli_close($db);
  } else {
    echo 'Connection failed.';
  }
?>
```

*Retrieving the ID of the Previously Inserted Item with MySQL
(mysqli_commit.php; excerpt)*

By default, MySQL statements you send to the database are executed immediately; this mode is also called autocommit. Recent MySQL versions also support transactions, which means that several SQL statements can be "bundled" into one statement. When you are working with transactions, either the whole transaction runs through, or none of it; a partial execution cannot happen.

To use transactions, first disable autocommit (with the `mysqli_autocommit()` function, for example) and from then on all SQL statements on the used connection will be part of the transaction. With `mysqli_commit()`, the statements are finally executed, and `mysqli_rollback()` puts the database back to the state without the transaction. At the end of the script, all pending transactions are committed automatically, but for performance purposes you should call `mysqli_commit()` as soon as possible.

9

Working with Other Databases

Apart from MySQL, PHP supports almost all relevant (and some not-so-relevant ones, as well) databases on Earth. This chapter features the basic techniques used with many of those systems, especially connecting to the database, executing SQL statements, and retrieving the return data. As in Chapter 8, "Working with MySQL Databases," we are using a sample database called **phrasebook** and a sample schema/table from within it called **quotes**, with the following four fields:

- **id**—An integer value that is increased by one for each new entry entered into the database. Depending on the database system, the data type is either called IDENTITY, auto_increment, or something similar.

- **quote**—The quote, as a VARCHAR(255); this length works with all systems.

- **author**—The person who produced the quote, as a VARCHAR(50).

- **year**—The year the quote was produced, of type INT.

Connecting to SQLite

```
@sqlite_open('quotes.db', 0666, $error)
$db = new SQLite3('quotes.db');
```

```php
<?php
  if ($db = @sqlite_open('quotes.db', 0666, $error))
➥{
    echo 'Connected to the database.';
    sqlite_close($db);
  } else {
    echo 'Connection failed: ' .
➥htmlspecialchars($error);
  }
?>
```

Connecting to SQLite (sqlite_open.php)

Starting with PHP 5, SQLite is bundled with the scripting language. This is a lightweight, file-based database. That allows very fast reading (in many cases, even faster than when using a "real" database), but writing can sometimes take longer than with other systems because file locking is an issue. However, PHP 4 users can also use SQLite because a PECL (PHP Extension Community Library) module is available (http://pecl.php.net/).

If you use PHP 5.0-5.3, SQLite support is already included. In PHP 5.4, the SQLite extension (ext/sqlite) has been moved to PECL. As an alternative, PHP 5.4 (and PHP 5.3, as well) offers the ext/sqlite3 extension, which is also covered in this chapter.

Windows users have to use (or compile) php_sqlite.dll, copy it to PHP's extension folder, and then load it using extension=php_sqlite.dll in their php.ini for ext/sqlite or extension=php_sqlite3.dll for ext/sqlite3.

When using ext/sqlite, you can connect to a SQLite data source using sqlite_open(). As the first parameter, you provide the name of the database file; it gets created if it doesn't exist yet. For this to work, the PHP process needs read and write privileges to the file. The second parameter is the file open mode (0666 is recommended); however, as of this writing, this parameter is ignored. The third parameter is a variable that contains any error messages (such as insufficient rights).

NOTE: Just like ext/mysqli, the SQLite extension under PHP 5 can also be accessed using an object-oriented programming (OOP) approach:

```php
<?php
  $db = new SQLiteDatabase('quotes.db');
  echo 'Connected to the database.';
  $db->close();
?>
```

For the sake of backward compatibility, this chapter uses the functional approach for the subsequent phrases.

The ext/sqlite3 extension uses a mandatory OOP application programming interface (API). Here, the open() method of the SQLite3 class would open a database file. Because you need to instantiate that class anyway, a quicker approach is to provide the filename in the class constructor, which in turn would open the

database, as well. Error handling could be achieved with
a try-catch-block:

```php
<?php
  try {
    $db = new SQLite3('quotes.db');
    echo 'Connected to the database.';
    $db->close();
  } catch ($ex) {
    echo 'An error has occurred.';
  }
?>
```

Connecting to SQLite3 (sqlite3_open.php)

Sending SQL to SQLite

```
sqlite_exec()
$db->exec()
```

```php
<?php
  if ($db = @sqlite_open('quotes.db', 0666, $error))
➥{
    sqlite_exec($db, sprintf(
      'INSERT INTO quotes (quote, author, year)
VALUES (\'%s\', \'%s\', \'%s\')',
      sqlite_escape_string($_POST['quote']),
      sqlite_escape_string($_POST['author']),
      intval($_POST['year'])));
    echo 'Quote saved.';
    sqlite_close($db);
  } else {
    echo 'Connection failed: ' .
➥htmlspecialchars($error);
  }
?>
```

Sending SQL to SQLite (sqlite_exec.php; excerpt)

The PHP function `sqlite_exec()` sends a SQL statement to the database using `ext/sqlite`. As the first parameter, the database handle—returned by `sqlite_open()`—is used; the second parameter is the SQL string. To avoid SQL injection, the PHP function `sqlite_escape_string()` escapes dangerous characters in dynamic data. The preceding code implements this for the sample table `quotes` that have also been used in the MySQL phrases in Chapter 8.

Users of `ext/sqlite3` need to execute the `exec()` method of the `SQLite3` class:

```php
<?php
  try {
    $db = new SQLite3('quotes.db');
    $db->exec(sprintf(
      'INSERT INTO quotes (quote, author, year)
➥VALUES (\'%s\', \'%s\', \'%s\')',
      $db->escape_string($_POST['quote']),
      $db->escape_string($_POST['author']),
      intval($_POST['year'])));
    echo 'Quote saved.';
    $db->close();
  } catch ($ex) {
    echo 'An error has occurred.';
  }
?>
```

Sending SQL to SQLite3 (sqlite3_exec.php; excerpt)

TIP: If a table contains an identity column (data type `INTEGER PRIMARY KEY` when using SQLite), calling the `sqlite_last_insert_rowid()` function (for `ext/sqlite`) or the `lastInsertRowID()` method (for `ext/sqlite3`) after sending a SQL statement returns the value this column has for the new entry in the database.

Retrieving Results of a Query to SQLite

```
$result = sqlite_query($db, 'SELECT * FROM quotes');
sqlite_fetch_array($result);
$result = $db->query('SELECT * FROM quotes');
$result->fetchArray();
```

```php
<table>
<tr><th>#</th><th>Quote</th><th>Author</th><th>Year
➡</th></tr>
<?php
  try {
    $db = new SQLite3('quotes.db');
    $result = $db->query('SELECT * FROM quotes');
    while ($row = $result->fetchArray($result)) {
      printf(
        '<tr><td>%s</td><td>%s</td><td>%s</td><td>%s
➡</td></tr>',
        htmlspecialchars($row['id']),
        htmlspecialchars($row['quote']),
        htmlspecialchars($row['author']),
        htmlspecialchars($row['year'])
      );
    }
    $db->close();
  } catch ($ex) {
    echo 'An error has occurred.';
  }
?>
</table>
```

Retrieving Data from SQLite3 (sqlite3_fetch.php; excerpt)

The function sqlite_exec() and method exec() from
the previous phrase are very quick performing; however,

it is not possible to access return values from the SQL statement sent with it. For this, `sqlite_query()` (ext/sqlite) or `query()` (ext/sqlite3) must be used. This function or method returns a handle of the resultset of the query. The following functions and methods can then be used to iterate over the resultset:

- The `sqlite_fetch_arrray()` function and `fetchArray()` method return the current row in the resultset as an associative array (field names become keys) and moves farther to the next row.

- `sqlite_fetch_object()` (no equivalent exists for ext/sqlite3) returns the current row in the result-set as an object (field names become properties) and moves farther to the next row.

- `sqlite_fetch_all()` (again, no equivalent exists for ext/sqlite3) returns the complete resultset as an array of associative arrays.

The preceding listing shows how to access all data within the resultset using the `fetchArray()` method; the following code does roughly the same, this time with `sqlite_fetch_object()`. A while loop calls this method or function as long as it returns something other than `false` (which means that there is no data left):

```
<table>
<tr><th>#</th><th>Quote</th><th>Author</th><th>Year
➥</th></tr>
<?php
  if ($db = @sqlite_open('quotes.db', 0666, $error))
➥{
    $result = sqlite_query($db, 'SELECT * FROM
➥quotes');
    while ($row = sqlite_fetch_object($result)) {
      printf(
```

```
        '<tr><td>%s</td><td>%s</td><td>%s</td><td>%s
➥</td></tr>',
        htmlspecialchars($row->id),
        htmlspecialchars($row->quote),
        htmlspecialchars($row->author),
        htmlspecialchars($row->year)
     );
   }
   sqlite_close($db);
 } else {
   printf('<tr><td colspan="4">Connection failed:
➥%s</td></tr>',
      htmlspecialchars($error));
 }
?>
</table>
```

Retrieving Data from SQLite (sqlite_fetch.php; excerpt)

TIP: Using sqlite_fetch_all() reads the whole result-set into memory simultaneously, if you are using ext/sqlite; ext/sqlite3 does not support this feature. So, if you do not have much data, this is the best-performing method. If you have more data, an iterative approach using sqlite_fetch_array() and sqlite_fetch_object() might be better.

Using Prepared Statements with SQLite

```
$stmt = $db->prepare('INSERT INTO quotes (quote,
➥author, year) VALUES (:quote, :author, :year)');
$stmt->bindValue(':quote', $_POST['quote']);
```

```php
<?php
  try {
    $db = new SQLite3('quotes.db');
    $stmt = $db->prepare('INSERT INTO quotes (quote,
➥author, year) VALUES (:quote, :author, :year)');
    $stmt->bindValue(':quote', $_POST['quote'],
➥SQLITE3_TEXT);
    $stmt->bindValue(':author', $_POST['author'],
➥SQLITE3_TEXT);
    $stmt->bindValue(':year',
➥intval($_POST['year']), SQLITE3_INTEGER);
    $db->close();
  } catch ($ex) {
    echo 'An error has occurred.';
  }
?>
```

Retrieving Data from SQLite3 (sqlite3_fetch.php; excerpt)

Prepared statements separate SQL commands from data by supporting placeholders within SQL. In a second step, values can be assigned to those placeholders.

When using ext_sqlite3, prepared statements can be used. In the first step, the prepare() method creates a SQLite3Stmt object representing a statement. Placeholders are denoted by a colon and the placeholder's name:

```php
$stmt = $db->prepare('INSERT INTO quotes (quote,
➥author, year) VALUES (:quote, :author, :year)');
```

Then, the statement object's bindValue() method assigns a value to a specific placeholder. You provide the name of the placeholder, the value to be assigned, and the data type to be used:

```php
$stmt->bindValue(':quote', $_POST['quote'],
➥SQLITE3_TEXT);
```

Currently, ext/sqlite3 supports these data types:

- **SQLITE3_BLOB**—BLOB data (binary large object)
- **SQLITE3_FLOAT**—A float value
- **SQLITE3_INTEGER**—An integer value
- **SQLITE3_NULL**—A NULL value
- **SQLITE3_TEXT**—A string

NOTE: The bindValue() method binds the value you provide to the placeholder. Instead, you could also use the bindParam() method, which binds the parameter you provide to the statement placeholder. Note that in that case you cannot use a value, because you need to provide a parameter that may be passed by reference. The following code would not work:

```
$stmt->bindParam(':year', 2012, SQLITE3_INTEGER);
```

Connecting to PostgreSQL

@pg_connect()

```php
<?php
  if ($db = @pg_connect('host=localhost port=5432
➥dbname=phrasebook user=postgres password=abc123'))
➥{
    echo 'Connected to the database.';
    pg_close($db);
  } else {
    echo 'Connection failed.';
  }
?>
```

Connecting to PostgreSQL (pg_connect.php)

PostgreSQL has a growing fan base. Some even say this is because with version 8.0 finally came a native Windows version. However, most production systems that use PostgreSQL are hosted on Linux or UNIX, nevertheless.

After you install the database, you can use Web-based administration software such as phpPgAdmin (http://sourceforge.net/projects/phppgadmin) or other tools such as the graphical user interface (GUI) application pgAdmin (www.pgadmin.org/) to administer the database. Alternatively, you can use the command-line tool. To allow PHP to access the PostgreSQL installation, Windows users must load the extension with the entry extension (`php_pgsql.dll`) in `php.ini`; UNIX/Linux users configure PHP with the switch `--with-pgsql=/path/to/pgsql`.

Then, `pg_connect()` connects to the data source. You have to provide a connection string that contains all important data, including host, port, name of the database, and user credentials.

Sending SQL to PostgreSQL

`pg_query()`

```php
<?php
  if ($db = @pg_connect('host=localhost port=5432
➥dbname=phrasebook user=postgres password=abc123'))
➥{
    pg_query($db, sprintf(
      'INSERT INTO quotes (quote, author, year)
➥VALUES (\'%s\', \'%s\', \'%s\')',
        pg_escape_string($_POST['quote']),
        pg_escape_string($_POST['author']),
        intval($_POST['year'])));
```

```
    echo 'Quote saved.';
    pg_close($db);
  } else {
    echo 'Connection failed.';
  }
?>
```

Sending SQL to PostgreSQL (pg_query.php; excerpt)

The function pg_query() sends SQL to the PostgreSQL installation. Again, escaping potentially dangerous characters such as single quotes is a must; this can be done with the pg_escape_string() function. In this code, you see the PHP portion of the script that accepts funny (or not-so-funny) phrases in an HTML form and writes them to the database.

NOTE: Retrieving the value in the identity column after the last INSERT statement is a bit tricky. The PostgreSQL term for such a data type is SERIAL, which automatically creates a sequence. To get the sequence's value, you can use pg_last_oid() to retrieve the oid (object id) of this value. Then, execute a SELECT id FROM quotes WHERE oid=<oid>, when <oid> is the oid you just retrieved. This then returns the desired value.

Updating Data in PostgreSQL

pg_insert()

```php
<?php
  if ($db = @pg_connect('host=localhost port=5432
➥dbname=phrasebook user=postgres password=abc123')) {
```

```
    $data = array(
        'quote' => pg_escape_string($_POST['quote']),
        'author' =>
➥pg_escape_string($_POST['author']),
        'year' => intval($_POST['year'])
    );
    pg_insert($db, 'quotes', $data);
    echo 'Quote saved.';
    pg_close($db);
  } else {
    echo 'Connection failed.';
  }
?>
```

Sending SQL to PostgreSQL (pg_insert.php; excerpt)

Another way to insert or update data in PostgreSQL
comes in the form of the functions pg_insert() and
pg_update(). The first parameter must be the database
handle, the second parameter is the table to be inserted
into/updated, and the third parameter contains some
data in the form of an associative array. (Column names
are the keys.) In the event of an UPDATE SQL statement,
the update condition must also be submitted as an
array in the fourth parameter of the function. The preceding code shows how to insert data.

Retrieving Results of a Query to PostgreSQL

```
$result = pg_query();
pg_fetch_row($result);
```

```
<table>
<tr><th>#</th><th>Quote</th><th>Author</th><th>Year
➥</th></tr>
<?php
  if ($db = @pg_connect('host=localhost port=5432
➥dbname=phrasebook user=postgres password=abc123'))
➥{
    $result = pg_query($db, 'SELECT * FROM quotes');
    while ($row = pg_fetch_row($result)) {
      vprintf(
        '<tr><td>%s</td><td>%s</td><td>%s</td><td>%s
➥</td></tr>',
        $row
      );
    }
    pg_close($db);
  } else {
    echo '<tr><td colspan="4">Connection
➥failed.</td></tr>';
  }
?>
</table>
```

Retrieving Data from PostgreSQL (pg_fetch.php; excerpt)

The return value of a call to pg_query() is a pointer to
a resultset that can be used with these functions:

- pg_fetch_assoc() returns the current row in the
  resultset as an associative array.

- pg_fetch_object() returns the current row in the
  resultset as an object.

- pg_fetch_row() returns the current row in the
  resultset as a numeric array.

- pg_fetch_all() returns the complete resultset as an
  array of associative arrays.

The preceding code uses `pg_fetch_row()` to read out all data from the `quotes` table.

Alternatively, `pg_select()` works similarly to `pg_insert()` and `pg_update()`. Just provide a database handle, a table name, and maybe a WHERE clause in the form of an array, and you get the complete resultset as an array of (associative) arrays:

```
$data = pg_select($db, 'quotes');
```

Connecting to Oracle

`@oci_connect()`

```php
<?php
  if ($db = @oci_connect('scott', 'tiger', 'orcl'))
➡{
    echo 'Connected to the database.';
    oci_close($db);
  } else {
    echo 'Connection failed.';
  }
?>
```

Connecting to Oracle (oci_connect.php)

Two PHP extensions are available for Oracle, but only one is actively maintained and also works with more recent versions of the relationship database management system (RDBMS). To install it, configure PHP with the switch `--with--oci8`. The environment variable `ORACLE_HOME` must be set so that PHP can find the client libraries. Windows users need the `php.ini` directive `extension=php_oci8.dll`. In addition, PHP requires read access to the client libraries (which need to be

installed separately). Then, oci_connect() tries to estab-
lish a connection to the server. The order of the parameters is a bit strange: first username and password and
then the name of the service (that has been configured
using the configuration assistant or is part of the
tnsnames.ora file). The return value is a handle to the
connection and is required by further operations in the
database.

Sending SQL to Oracle

```
oci_execute()
```

```php
<?php
  if ($db = @oci_connect('scott', 'tiger', 'orcl'))
➡{
    require_once 'stripFormSlashes.inc.php';
    $sql = 'INSERT INTO quotes (quote, author, year)
➡VALUES (:quote, :author, :year)';
    $stmt = oci_parse($db, $sql);
    oci_bind_by_name($stmt, ':quote',
➡$_POST['quote']);
    oci_bind_by_name($stmt, ':author',
$_POST['author']);
    oci_bind_by_name($stmt, ':year',
➡intval($_POST['year']));
    oci_execute($stmt, OCI_COMMIT_ON_SUCCESS);
    echo 'Quote saved.';
    oci_close($db);
  } else {
    echo 'Connection failed.';
  }
?>
```

Sending SQL to Oracle (oci_execute.php; excerpt)

This section again uses the `quotes` table, which also includes an identity column; however, this is a bit more complicated to implement with Oracle. Refer to the script `quotes.oracle.sql` in the download archive for more information.

To send SQL to Oracle, two steps are required. First, a call to `oci_parse()` parses a SQL string and returns a resource that can then be executed using `oci_execute()`. The second parameter of `oci_execute()` is quite important. Several constants are allowed, but most of the time, `OCI_DEFAULT` is used. Despite the name, that's not the default value, but means "no auto-commit." In contrast, `OCI_COMMIT_ON_SUCCESS` commits the pending transaction when no error has occurred. And this is, indeed, the default value.

Unfortunately, there is no such thing as `oci_escape_string()` to escape special characters for use in a SQL statement. Therefore, prepared statements are a must—but are also very easy to implement. For this, the SQL statement must contain placeholders that start with a colon:

```
$sql = 'INSERT INTO quotes (quote, author, year)
➥VALUES (:quote, :author, :year)';
```

Then, these placeholders have to be filled with values. For this, `oci_bind_by_name()` must be used:

```
oci_bind_by_name($stmt, ':quote', $_POST['quote']);
```

The preceding code sends some form data to the database. No need to worry about special characters because `oci_bind_by_name()` takes care of that.

NOTE: When you are using OCI_DEFAULT as the commit mode, the changes must be written to the database using oci_commit($db); oci_rollback($db) performs a rollback.

TIP: By the way, if you want to retrieve the autovalue of the most recent INSERT operation, you have to do it within a transaction and execute SELECT quotes_id.CURVAL AS id FROM DUAL, where quotes_id is the name of the sequence you are using.

Retrieving Results of a Query to Oracle

```
oci_fetch_object($stmt)
```

```
<table>
<tr><th>#</th><th>Quote</th><th>Author</th><th>Year
➥</th></tr>
<?php
  if ($db = @oci_connect('scott', 'tiger', 'orcl'))
➥{
    $stmt = oci_parse($db, 'SELECT * FROM quotes');
    oci_execute($stmt, OCI_COMMIT_ON_SUCCESS);
    while ($row = oci_fetch_object($stmt)) {
      printf(
        '<tr><td>%s</td><td>%s</td><td>%s</td><td>%s
➥</td></tr>',
        htmlspecialchars($row->ID),
        htmlspecialchars($row->QUOTE),
        htmlspecialchars($row->AUTHOR),
```

```
        htmlspecialchars($row->YEAR)
      );
    }
    oci_close($db);
  } else {
    echo '<tr><td colspan="4">Connection
➥failed.</td></tr>';
  }
?>
</table>
```

Retrieving Data from Oracle (oci_fetch.php; excerpt)

You have several ways to access the return values of a SQL query, but the following functions are used most often in practice:

- `oci_fetch_assoc()` returns the current row in the resultset as an associative array.

- `oci_fetch_object()` returns the current row in the resultset as an object.

- `oci_fetch_row()` returns the current row in the resultset as a numeric array.

- `oci_fetch_all()` returns the complete resultset as an array of associative arrays. However, five parameters are required: the statement object from `oci_parse()`, the array that is used for the return data, the number of lines to skip, the maximum number of rows to be returned (-1 means infinite), and whether to return a numeric (`OCI_NUM`) or associative (`OCI_ASSOC`) array.

The listing in this phrase uses a `while` loop and `oci_fetch_object()` to retrieve all data in the table.

NOTE: Oracle always returns column names in upper-case. Therefore, you have to use uppercase object properties or uppercase associative array keys when accessing the return values of a SQL query.

Connecting to MSSQL

```
@sqlsrv_connect()
```

```php
<?php
  $config = array('UID' => 'user', 'PWD' =>
➥'password', 'Database' => 'phrasebook');
  if ($db = @sqlsrv_connect('(local)\SQLEXPRESS',
➥$config)) {
    echo 'Connected to the database.';
    sqlsrv_close($db);
  } else {
    echo 'Connection failed.';
  }
?>
```

Connecting to MSSQL (sqlsrv_connect.php)

The Microsoft SQL engine comes in two flavors: the fully featured (and fully priced) Microsoft SQL Server (short: MSSQL) and the free edition, the Microsoft SQL Server Express Edition, available for free at www.microsoft.com/sqlserver/en/us/editions/express.aspx. Both versions are supported by PHP because they are compatible with each other.

PHP ships with an extension for MSSQL, ext/mssql. However it is quite old and not actively maintained anymore. Instead, Microsoft provides a new (Windows-only) extension, `ext/sqlsrv`, which is the recommended one to use.

To make it work, you need to add the extension using `extension=<filename>.dll` in your `php.ini`. Also, you need the extension itself. Depending on which version of PHP you are using, you need a specific version. The PHP manual page http://php.net/sqlsrv.installation points you to the correct download page. If possible, you should use at least version 3 of the extension, which uses the Microsoft SQL Server 2012 Native Client libraries; version 2 requires the Microsoft SQL Server 2008 R2 Native Client libraries. Microsoft describes the up-to-date system requirements at http://msdn.microsoft.com/en-us/library/cc296170.aspx.

To connect to MSSQL, call `mssql_connect()` and provide the name of the server (`(local)` serves as shortcut for `localhost`); if you are using a named instance of Microsoft SQL Server (for example, `SQLEXPRESS`, which is installed with the MSSQL Express Edition by default), you append it to the server name, separated by a backslash: `(local)\SQLEXPRESS`. As the second argument, you can provide an array with connection information. The following array keys are supported by the extension:

- **Database**—Name of the database
- **PWD**—Password
- **UID**—Username

If you want to authenticate against the database with the current user (sometimes also called *trusted connection*), just omit the `UID` and `PWD` configuration settings.

Sending SQL to MSSQL

```
sqlsrv_query()
```

```php
<?php
  $config = array('UID' => 'user', 'PWD' =>
➥'password', 'Database' => 'phrasebook');
  if ($db = @sqlsrv_connect('(local)\SQLEXPRESS',
➥$config)) {
    ini_set('magic_quotes_sybase', 'On');
    sqlsrv_query($db, sprintf(
      'INSERT INTO quotes (quote, author, year)
➥VALUES (\'%s\', \'%s\', \'%s\')',
      addslashes($_POST['quote']),
      addslashes($_POST['author']),
      intval($_POST['year'])));
    echo 'Quote saved.';
    sqlsrv_close($db);
  } else {
    echo 'Connection failed.';
  }
?>
```

Sending SQL to MSSQL (sqlsrv_execute.php; excerpt)

The function sqlsrv_query() sends a SQL statement to the MSSQL installation. The parameter order is similar to the one from ext/mysqli: first the database handle, then the SQL command.

Another important point is escaping special characters. In MSSQL, single quotes must not be escaped using a backslash, but double quotes are the way to go:

```
INSERT INTO quotes (quote, author, year) VALUES
➥('Ain''t Misbehavin''', 'Louis Armstrong', 1929)
```

To achieve this, you can use addslashes(). However, first, you must configure it to behave so that MSSQL/MSDE-compatible strings are returned:

```
ini_set('magic_quotes_sybase', 'On');
$author = addslashes($_POST['author']);
```

One word of warning, though: The magic_quotes_sybase setting has been deprecated in PHP 5.3 and removed in PHP 5.4. If you are using user information in SQL statements, you should use prepared statements instead (two phrases onward).

The listing at the beginning of this phrase sanitizes some form data and writes it to the (by now) well-known sample database.

Retrieving Results of a Query to MSSQL

```
$result = sqlsrv_query();
sqlsrv_fetch_object($result);
```

```
<table>
<tr><th>#</th><th>Quote</th><th>Author</th><th>Year
➥</th></tr>
<?php
  $config = array('UID' => 'user', 'PWD' =>
➥'password', 'Database' => 'phrasebook');
  if ($db = @sqlsrv_connect('(local)\SQLEXPRESS',
➥$config)) {
    $result = sqlsrv_query($db, 'SELECT * FROM
➥quotes');
    while ($obj = sqlsrv_fetch_object($result)) {
      printf(
```

```
        '<tr><td>%s</td><td>%s</td><td>%s</td><td>%s
➥</td></tr>',
        htmlspecialchars($row->id),
        htmlspecialchars($row->quote),
        htmlspecialchars($row->author),
        htmlspecialchars($row->year)
    );
  }
  sqlsrv_close($db);
} else {
  echo '<tr><td colspan="4">Connection
➥failed.</td></tr>';
  }
?>
</table>
```

Retrieving Data from MSSQL (sqlsrv_fetch.php; excerpt)

Finally, there is, of course, a way to retrieve all data in the resultset. A while loop comes into play, using one of these functions:

- sqlsrv_fetch_array() returns the current row in the resultset as an associative array and/or a numerically indexed array; by default, it returns both.

- sqlsrv_fetch_object() returns the current row in the resultset as an object.

Using Prepared Statements with MSSQL

```
$stmt = sqlsrv_query();
sqlsrv_execute($stmt);
```

```php
<?php
  $config = array('UID' => 'user', 'PWD' =>
➥'password', 'Database' => 'phrasebook');
  if ($db = @sqlsrv_connect('(local)\SQLEXPRESS',
$config)) {
    $year_as_int = intval($_POST['year']);
    $data = array(&$_POST['quote'],
➥&$_POST['author'], &$year_as_int);
    $stmt = sqlsrv_query(
      $db,
      'INSERT INTO quotes (quote, author, year)
➥VALUES (?, ?, ?)',
      $data);
    sqlsrv_execute($stmt);
    echo 'Quote saved.';
    sqlsrv_close($db);
  } else {
    echo 'Connection failed.';
  }
?>
```

*Retrieving Data from MSSQL with Prepared Statements
(sqlsrv_prepare.php; excerpt)*

Because there is no designated escaping functions in
ext/sqlsrv, prepared statements are the only viable way
to use user-supplied data in SQL statements and to
avoid SQL injection. As usual, two steps must be taken.
First, you create a statement object (the function to be
used here is sqlsrv_prepare()) with placeholders, and
then you execute this statement. While preparing the
statement, you also have to provide the data for the
placeholders.

The ext/sqlsrv extensions expects a question mark (?)
for each placeholder. The values for those placeholders
are provided in an array, in the exact order as the placeholders in the SQL statement. These values can be
passed by reference.

Using MSSQL without Windows

```
$db = @mssql_connect();
$result = mssql_query();
mssql_fetch_assoc($result);
```

```
<table>
<tr><th>#</th><th>Quote</th><th>Author</th><th>Year
➥</th></tr>
<?php
  if ($db = @mssql_connect('localhost', 'user',
➥'password')) {
    mssql_select_db('phrasebook', $db);
    $result = mssql_query('SELECT * FROM quotes',
➥$db);
    while ($row = mssql_fetch_assoc($result)) {
      printf(
        '<tr><td>%s</td><td>%s</td><td>%s</td><td>%s
➥</td></tr>',
        htmlspecialchars($row['id']),
        htmlspecialchars($row['quote']),
        htmlspecialchars($row['author']),
        htmlspecialchars($row['year'])
      );
    }
    mssql_close($db);
  } else {
    echo '<tr><td colspan="4">Connection
➥failed.</td></tr>';
  }
?>
</table>
```

Retrieving Data from MSSQL with ext/mssql (mssql_fetch.php; excerpt)

There is one remaining reason to use the deprecated
ext/mssql extension: In a heterogeneous network,
UNIX/Linux systems can access MSSQL installations
and connect to them using the old MSSQL extension.
For this to work, you have to download the FreeTDS
library from www.freetds.org/ and install it after
unpacking the distribution with this command:

```
./configure --prefix=/usr/local/tds --with-tdsver=4.2
make
sudo make install
```

Then, reconfigure PHP with the switch
--with-sybase=/usr/local/freetds.

Finally, you can connect to the server using
mssql_connect() and select the database to be used
using mssql_select_db(), similar to the API used by
other database extensions. After executing a SQL query
with mssql_query(), you can retrieve return data with
one of the following functions:

- mssql_fetch_assoc() returns the current row in the
  resultset as an associative array.

- mssql_fetch_object() returns the current row in
  the resultset as an object.

- mssql_fetch_row() returns the current row in the
  resultset as a numeric array.

NOTE: MSSQL supports two modes to authenticate
users: SQL authentication and Windows authentication.
The latter checks whether the current Windows user
has sufficient rights to access the database. In a con-
trolled environment, this might be a better idea than
using username and password. However, you first have
to find out which user is used. For instance, Microsoft
Internet Information Services (IIS) Web server software

normally uses the Internet guest account (that is, IUSR_<machinename>). Therefore, this user requires privileges in the database.

To use Windows authentication—sometimes also called trusted connection—you need the following php.ini directive:

```
mssql.secure_connection = On
```

Connecting to Firebird

```
ibase_connect()
```

```php
<?php
  if ($db =
➥ibase_connect('localhost:/tmp/quotes.gdb', 'user',
➥'password')) {
    echo 'Connected to the database.';
    ibase_close($db);
  } else {
    echo 'Connection failed.';
  }
?>
```

Connecting to InterBase/Firebird (ibase_connect.php)

The Firebird database is currently more an insider's tip than a widely in use database, but it is getting more users and may be an alternative to an established RDBMS. The origins of this database lie in Borland's InterBase product. Therefore, the extension is called ibase or interbase. So, Windows users need extension=php_interbase.dll in their php.ini, whereas "self-compilers" must configure PHP with the switch --with-interbase=/path/to/firebird. Then, Firebird supports two modes: a file mode comparable to

SQLite and a server mode. For the sake of interoperability and for an easy deployment, this section uses the file mode.

This section also uses `.gdb` files that are compatible with both Firebird and InterBase; the new Firebird format has the extension `.fdb`. After this file is created, `ibase_connect()` connects to the file or database. For the host, you have to provide a string in the format `'localhost:/path/to/file.gdb'` when using TCP/IP or the local filename (the listings assume that the file resides in `/tmp` on the local machine); you also need a username and a password.

Sending SQL to Firebird

```php
ibase_execute()

<?php
  if ($db =
➥ibase_connect('localhost:/tmp/quotes.gdb', 'user',
➥'password')) {
    require_once 'stripFormSlashes.inc.php';
    $sql = 'INSERT INTO quotes (id, quote, author,
➥qyear) ' .
      'VALUES (GEN_ID(quotes_gen, 1), ?, ?, ?)';
    $stmt = ibase_prepare($db, $sql);
    ibase_execute($stmt,
      $_POST['quote'], $_POST['author'],
➥intval($_POST['year']));
    echo 'Quote saved.';
    ibase_close($db);
  } else {
    echo 'Connection failed.';
  }
?>
```

Sending SQL to InterBase/Firebird (ibase_execute.php; excerpt)

The function ibase_query() can be used to send a SQL string to the database. However, there is no ibase_escape_string(); so, to be safe from SQL injection, a prepared statement must be used. Here, the function ibase_prepare() comes into play: It parses a SQL statement (with question marks as placeholders) and returns a statement object. Then, ibase_execute() executes this statement and retrieves the values for the placeholders as additional parameters.

NOTE: The preceding code contains two specialities of Firebird. First, the identity column is driven by a generator in the database; the call to GEN_ID(quotes_gen, 1) enters the next available value in this column when inserting a new field. Also, the word year is reserved within Firebird, so the column's name is qyear.

Retrieving Results of a Query to Firebird

```
$result = ibase_query();
ibase fetch object($result);
```

```
<table>
<tr><th>#</th><th>Quote</th><th>Author</th><th>Year
➥</th></tr>
<?php
  if ($db = ibase_connect('//CHRISTIAN2003/
➥tmp/quotes.gdb', 'user', 'password')) {
    $result = ibase_query($db, 'SELECT * FROM
➥quotes');
    while ($row = ibase_fetch_object($result)) {
      printf(
```

```
      '<tr><td>%s</td><td>%s</td><td>%s</td><td>%s
➥</td></tr>',
      htmlspecialchars($row->ID),
      htmlspecialchars($row->QUOTE),
      htmlspecialchars($row->AUTHOR),
      htmlspecialchars($row->QYEAR)
    );
  }
  ibase_close($db);
} else {
  echo '<tr><td colspan="4">Connection
➥failed.</td></tr>';
  }
?>
</table>
```

Retrieving Data from InterBase/Firebird (ibase_fetch.php; excerpt)

No matter whether you are using ibase_query or ibase_execute(), at the end, you have a handle for the resultset, which you can iterate with ibase_fetch_assoc() (which returns an associative array) or ibase_fetch_object() (which returns an object). This code uses the latter method.

Keep in mind that Firebird and InterBase return column names in uppercase, so the object properties (and the keys in the associative arrays) are uppercase, too.

Connecting via PDO

```
try {
  $db = new PDO('sqlite:PDOquotes.db');
  }
```

```php
<?php
  try {
    $db = new PDO('sqlite:PDOquotes.db');
    echo 'Connected to the database.';
  } catch (PDOException $ex) {
    echo 'Connection failed: ' .
➥htmlspecialchars($ex->getMessage());
  }
?>
```

Connecting via PDO (pdo_connect.php)

A new development from some core PHP developers
and one of the key features of PHP 5.1 has been PDO,
short for PHP Data Objects. There are several abstraction classes in PHP, but PDO will eventually become
the official one. As of PHP 5.3, PDO is part of the
PHP core, so Windows users do not need to reference
a specific DLL in php.ini. (In older PHP versions,
extension=php_pdo.dll does the trick.)

Apart from having access to PDO itself, a driver for the
database to be used must be loaded, as well. As of this
writing, the following drivers are available:

- PDO_CUBRID for Cubrid
- PDO_DBLIB for Microsoft SQL Server (based on the
  old ext/mssql extension)
- PDO_FIREBIRD for InterBase/Firebird
- PDO_IBM for DB2
- PDO_INFORMIX for Informix
- PDO_MYSQL for MySQL 3.x–5.x
- PDO_OCI for Oracle
- PDO_ODBC for ODBC

- PDO_PGSQL for PostgreSQL
- PDO_SQLITE for SQLite versions 2 and 3
- PDO_SQLSRV for Microsoft SQL Server (based on the new ext/sqlsrv extension)
- PDO_4D for 4D

To make this as portable and easy to deploy as possible, the following phrases use the SQLite driver; however, other drivers and database systems are just as good. Whatever system you choose, download and install the driver in your php.ini. If you are using a PHP version earlier than PHP 5.3, make sure that you load the driver *after* PDO—in newer PHP versions, you do not need to specifically load PDO.

PDO exposes an object-oriented approach. All you need is a suitable data source name (DSN), a user, and a password (and possibly other options). The preceding code connects to/creates a SQLite version 3 file.

Sending SQL via PDO

```
$stmt = $db->prepare($sql);
$stmt->execute();
```

```php
<?php
  try {
    $db = new PDO('sqlite:PDOquotes.db');
    $sql = 'INSERT INTO quotes (quote, author, year)
➡VALUES (:quote, :author, :year)';
    $stmt = $db->prepare($sql);
    $stmt->bindValue('quote', $_POST['quote']);
    $stmt->bindValue('author', $_POST['author']);
    $stmt->bindValue('year',
➡intval($_POST['year']));
```

```
   $stmt->execute();
   echo 'Quote saved.';
  } catch (PDOException $ex) {
   echo 'Connection failed: ' .
►htmlspecialchars($ex->getMessage());
  }
?>
```

Sending SQL via PDO (pdo_execute.php; excerpt)

To send SQL via PDO, a statement must be executed
using the query() method. As always, you need a way to
escape special characters. This can, once again, be done
using prepared statements. First, a SQL query can be
parsed using a method called prepare(), whereas placeholders start with a colon. Then, the bindValue()
method binds a value to a placeholder name
(bindParam() would also work, but requires a value that
may be used by reference). Finally, the execute()
method sends the statement to the database.

Retrieving Results of a Query via PDO

```
$result = $db->query();
$result->fetch(PDO_FETCH_ASSOC);
```

```
<table>
<tr><th>#</th><th>Quote</th><th>Author</th><th>Year
►</th></tr>
<?php
  try {
    $db = new PDO('sqlite:PDOquotes.db');
    $result = $db->query('SELECT * FROM quotes');
    while ($row = $result->fetch(PDO_FETCH_ASSOC)) {
```

```
    printf(
      '<tr><td>%s</td><td>%s</td><td>%s</td><td>
➥%s</td></tr>',
      htmlspecialchars($row['id']),
      htmlspecialchars($row['quote']),
      htmlspecialchars($row['author']),
      htmlspecialchars($row['year'])
    );
  }
} catch (PDOException $ex) {
  echo 'Connection failed: ' .
➥htmlspecialchars($ex->getMessage());
  }
?>
</table>
```

Retrieving Data via PDO (pdo_fetch.php; excerpt)

Finally, reading out results from a SQL query with
PDO is done using the standard approach: Send the
SELECT query to the server and then use a while loop to
iterate over the results. Here, the iteration is done using
the fetch() method. You can provide as a parameter
constants such as PDO_FETCH_ASSOC (which returns an
associative array) or PDO_FETCH_OBJ (which returns an
object). Alternatively, you can use the fetchAll()
method and get an array of arrays so that you have all
the data at once.

This code uses fetch() and PDO_FETCH_ASSOC to read out
all data from the data source.

NOTE: As of this writing, PDO cannot be considered as
stable yet; therefore, it is possible that the API or
behavior of PDO may change in the future. Also, if you
try out PDO, be aware that this is still not proven to be
as reliable as PHP itself.

What Does PEAR Offer?

The following PHP Extension and Application Repository (PEAR) packages (among others) offer database abstraction layers and other goodies for database access:

- DB_DataObject can create SQL from objects.
- MDB_QueryTool offers some help for building SQL queries.
- MDB2 is a very feature-rich database abstraction layers.

If you are using a framework like Symfony or Zend Framework, you will have additional database access options there, as well.

10

Using XML

After the hype, the Extensible Markup Language (XML) is now really used almost everywhere. An application that receives a lot of buzz is Web Services, a technology that is covered in detail in Chapter 9, "Working with Other Databases." However, XML can be used elsewhere, as well. It is a good format to store any kind of data.

The tasks behind using XML are always the same: reading data from XML and writing data into it. So, this chapter focuses on these tasks and shows how to implement them.

Unfortunately, PHP 4's XML support was somewhat limited. Some extensions did not prove to be very stable. This changed drastically with PHP 5 and a revamped XML support. Therefore, we completely omit PHP 4 in this chapter (and in the rest of this book). In PHP 5.1 and 5.2, some new features have been added that are also covered in this chapter.

As the sample XML file and format in this chapter, the XML from the following code reuses the quotes database example from the preceding chapter. As you can see, `<quotes>` is the root element, and each quote

(including its author and the year the phrase was
coined) is contained in a `<quote>` element.

```xml
<?xml version="1.0" encoding="ISO-8859-1" ?>
<quotes>
  <quote year="1991">
    <phrase>Hasta la vista, baby!</phrase>
    <author>Arnold Schwarzenegger</author>
  </quote>
</quotes>
```

The Sample XML File (quotes.xml; excerpt)

Parsing XML with SAX

```php
$sax = xml_parser_create();
```

```php
$sax = xml_parser_create();
xml_parser_set_option($sax, XML_OPTION_CASE_FOLDING,
➥false);
xml_parser_set_option($sax, XML_OPTION_SKIP_WHITE,
true);
xml_set_element_handler($sax, 'sax_start',
➥'sax_end');
xml_set_character_data_handler($sax, 'sax_cdata');
xml_parse($sax, file_get_contents('quotes.xml'),
➥true);
xml_parser_free($sax);
```

Parsing XML with SAX (sax.php; excerpt)

Simple API for XML (SAX) is an approach to parse
XML documents, but not to validate them.

You create a SAX parser using xml_parser_create(), optionally providing the encoding as an argument. This parser can look at an XML file and react upon various events. The following three events are the most important ones:

- Beginning of an element
- End of an element
- CDATA blocks

You can then define handler functions for these elements and use them to transform the XML into something else, for instance Hypertext Markup Language (HTML). The following listing shows this and outputs the contents of the XML file as a bulleted HTML list, as shown in Figure 10.1. The function xml_set_element_handler() sets the handlers for the beginning and end of an element, whereas xml_set_character_data_handler() sets the handler for CDATA blocks. With xml_parser_set_option(), you can configure the handler, for instance, to ignore whitespace and to handle tag names as case sensitive (then tag names are not converted into uppercase letters automatically). The following code contains the code for the handler functions:

```
function sax_start($sax, $tag, $attr) {
  if ($tag == 'quotes') {
    echo '<ul>';
  } elseif ($tag == 'quote') {
    echo '<li>' . htmlspecialchars($attr['year']) .
': ';
  } elseif ($tag == 'phrase') {
    echo '"';
  } elseif ($tag == 'author') {
    echo ' (';
  }
```

```
}
function sax_end($sax, $tag) {
  if ($tag == 'quotes') {
    echo '</ul>';
  } elseif ($tag == 'quote') {
    echo '</li>';
  } elseif ($tag == 'phrase') {
    echo '"';
  } elseif ($tag == 'author') {
    echo ') ';
  }
}
function sax_cdata($sax, $data) {
  echo htmlspecialchars($data);
}
```

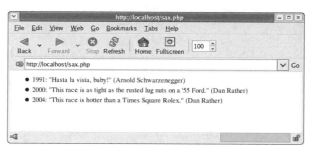

Figure 10.1   HTML created from XML

Parsing XML with XMLReader

```
$xml = new XMLReader();
```

```
echo '<ul>';
$xml = new XMLReader();
$xml->open('quotes.xml');
```

```
while ($xml->read()) {
  if ($xml->nodeType == XMLREADER::ELEMENT) {
    if ($xml->localName == 'phrase') {
      $xml->read();
      echo '<li>' . htmlspecialchars($xml->value) .
➥'</li>';
    }
  }
}
echo '</ul>';
```

Parsing XML with XMLReader (xmlreader.php)

XMLReader, a clone of the XmlTextReader interface in Microsoft .NET, became part of the PHP distribution with version 5.1.0 and is activated by default. At first glance, it looks similar to the SAX parser, but a fundamental difference exists: SAX is an event-based parser, whereas XMLReader uses a cursor that iterates over all elements in an XML file.

To user XMLReader, you instantiate the XMLReader class and then open a file (open() method). The common pattern used iterates over all elements using a while loop and the read() method.

Within that loop, you can determine the type of node the cursor has reached (noteTyp property) and then act accordingly (for instance, by reading out tag names [localName property] and accessing the value of text nodes [value property]).

The preceding code again reads in all phrases from the XML document and outputs them as a bulleted list.

Using DOM to Read XML

```php
$dom = new DOMDocument();
```

```php
<?php
  $dom = new DOMDocument();
  $dom->load('quotes.xml');
  echo '<ul>';
  foreach ($dom->getElementsByTagname('quote') as
➥$element) {
    $year = $element->getAttribute('year');
    foreach (($element->childNodes) as $e) {
      if ($e instanceof DOMElement) {
        if ($e->tagName == 'phrase') {
          $phrase = htmlspecialchars($e-
➥>textContent);
        } elseif ($e->tagName == 'author') {
          $author = htmlspecialchars($e-
➥>textContent);
        }
      }
    }
    echo "<li>$author: \"$phrase\" ($year)</li>";
  }
  echo '</ul>';
?>
```

Parsing XML with DOM (dom-read.php; excerpt)

The W3C's Document Object Model (DOM) defines a unified way to access elements in an XML structure. Therefore, accessing elements in an HTML page using JavaScript's DOM access and accessing elements in an XML file using PHP's DOM access are quite similar.

The DOM extension is bundled with PHP, so no installation is required. First, you instantiate a

`DOMDocument` object, and then you `load()` a file or
`loadXML()` a string. The new object supports, among
other functionality, the two methods
`getElementsByTagname()` and `getElementById()` that
return all nodes with a certain tag name or a specific
element identified by its ID. Then each node exposes
some properties such as the following:

- **firstChild**—First child node
- **lastChild**—Last child node
- **nextSibling**—Next node
- **previousSibling**—Previous node
- **nodeValue**—Value of the node

The preceding code uses DOM to access all quotes in
the XML file and outputs them.

Note that the listings use `instanceof` so that the tag
names are only evaluated in nodes of the type
`DOMElement`. This is because whitespace is considered as
a DOM node (however, of type `DOMText`).

Using DOM to Write XML

```
$dom->save('quotes.xml');
```

```php
<?php
  $dom = new DOMDocument();
  $dom->load('quotes.xml');
  $quote = $dom->createElement('quote');
  $quote->setAttribute('year', $_POST['year']);
  $phrase = $dom->createElement('phrase');
  $phraseText = $dom-
➥>createTextNode($_POST['quote']);
  $phrase->appendChild($phraseText);
```

```
  $author = $dom->createElement('author');
  $authorText = $dom-
➥>createTextNode($_POST['author']);
  $author->appendChild($authorText);
  $quote->appendChild($phrase);
  $quote->appendChild($author);
  $dom->documentElement->appendChild($quote);
  $dom->save('quotes.xml');
  echo 'Quote saved.';
?>
```

Creating XML with DOM (dom-write.php; excerpt)

Apart from the read access, it is also possible to build
complete XML documents from the ground up using
PHP's DOM support. This might look a bit clumsy, but
it works very well when you have to automatically
parse a lot of data.

The createElement() method creates a new element.
You can set its content by appending a new text node
(created with createTextNode()) and add attributes with
setAttribute(). Finally, you access the root element of
the XML file with documentElement and then call
appendChild(). Finally, save() writes the whole XML
file to the hard disk.

The preceding code saves author, quote, and year in an
XML document, appending to the data already there.

NOTE: PHP 5's DOM extension does not offer something like set_content() (which was available in PHP
4), so you have to define the text values of the nodes
using the createTextNode() method, as shown in the
preceding code.

Using XMLWriter to Write XML

```
$xml = new XMLWriter();
```

```php
<?php
  header('Content-type', 'text/xml; charset=
➡ISO-8859-1');

  $xml = new XMLWriter();
  $xml->openMemory();
  $xml->startDocument('1.0', 'ISO-8859-1');
  $xml->startElement('quotes');
    $xml->startElement('quote');
    $xml->writeAttribute('year', '1991');
      $xml->startElement('phrase');
      $xml->text('Hasta la vista, baby!');
      $xml->endElement();
      $xml->startElement('author');
      $xml->text('Arnold Schwarzenegger');
      $xml->endElement();
    $xml->endElement();
  $xml->endElement();
  $xml->endElement();
  echo $xml->outputMemory();
?>
```

Creating XML with XMLWriter (xmlwriter.php)

XMLWriter, the sibling of XMLReader, was introduced into the PHP distribution in version 5.1.2. It
provides a structured API to create XML files and is
especially valuable when you are dynamically creating
XML data (for instance, when processing data from a
database).

The API is quite simple: After opening an XML document in memory, you have specific functions to start the document, to start and end an element, and to write attributes and text nodes. The preceding code creates the XML file from the beginning of this chapter, except for the indentation; see Figure 10.2 for the result.

Figure 10.2   XML created with XMLWriter

Using SimpleXML

```
$xml = simplexml_load_file('quotes.xml');
```

```php
<?php
  $xml = simplexml_load_file('quotes.xml');
  echo '<ul>';
  foreach ($xml->quote as $quote) {
    $year = htmlspecialchars($quote['year']);
    $phrase = htmlspecialchars($quote->phrase);
    $author = htmlspecialchars($quote->author);
    echo "<li>$author: \"$phrase\" ($year)</li>";
  }
  echo '</ul>';
?>
```

Parsing XML with SimpleXML (simplexml-read.php)

One of the greatest new features in PHP 5.1 is the SimpleXML extension, an idea borrowed from a Perl module in CPAN. The approach is as simple as it is ingenious. The most intuitive way to access XML is probably via an object-oriented programming (OOP) approach: Subnodes are properties of their parent nodes/objects, and XML attributes turn into object attributes. This makes accessing XML very easy, including full iterator support, so `foreach` can be used.

This code loads a file using `simplexml_load_file()`—you can also use `simplexml_load_string()` for strings—and then reads all information in.

Compare this to the DOM approach. SimpleXML may be slower in some instances than DOM, but the coding is so much quicker.

NOTE: Writing can be done easily, as well. However, it is not possible to append elements without any external help (for instance, by using DOM and loading this DOM into SimpleXML using `simplexml_import_dom()`).

Using XPath with SimpleXML

```
$xml->xpath()
```

```php
<?php
  $xml = simplexml_load_file('quotes.xml');
  foreach ($xml->xpath('*/quote') as $quote) {
    echo '<p>' . htmlspecialchars($quote) . '</p>';
  }
?>
```

Using XPath with SimpleXML (xpath.php)

One of the best guarded secrets of SimpleXML is that the extension has a built-in support for XPath, the XML query language. Using it is easy: After creating a SimpleXML object, you can use the xpath() method and get all matching nodes in return.

Transforming XML with XSL

```
$xslt = new XsltProcessor();
```

```php
<?php
  $xml = new DOMDocument();
  $xml->load('quotes.xml');
  $xsl = new DOMDocument();
  $xsl->load('quotes.xsl');
  $xslt = new XsltProcessor();
  $xslt->importStylesheet($xsl);
  $result = $xslt->transformToDoc($xml);
  echo $result->saveXML();
?>
```

Using XSLT with PHP (xslt.php)

Transforming XML into another format is usually done by XSLT (XSL Transformation). In PHP, XSLT is done by libxslt and can be enabled using php_xsl.dll (in php.ini) on Windows and the switch --with-xsl on other platforms. Writing the XSL file may be hard, but the PHP code afterward is quite simple: Load both the XML and the XSLT (which is an XML document, as well) into a DOM object, and then instantiate an XsltProcessor object. Call importStylesheet(), and then transformToDoc().

The preceding phrase contains the code for these steps; the file quotes.xsl in the download repository contains markup that transforms the quotes' XML into the well-known HTML bulleted list.

Validating XML

```
$dom->relaxNGValidate('quotes.rng')
```

```php
<?php
  $dom = new DOMDocument;
  $dom->load('quotes.xml');
  echo 'Validation ' .
    (($dom->relaxNGValidate('quotes.rng')) ?
➥'succeeded.' : 'failed.');
?>
```

Validating XML against relaxNG (validate-rng.php)

PHP can validate XML against three types of files: Document Type Definitions (DTDs), Schemas (.xsd), and relaxNG. For the last two, the following four methods of the DOM object are available:

- **schemaValidate('file.xsd')**—Validates against a Schema file
- **schemaValidateSource('...')**—Validates against a Schema string
- **relaxNGValidate('file.rng')**—Validates against a relaxNG file
- **relaxNGValidateSource('...')**—Validates against a relaxNG string

The preceding code uses relaxNGValidate() to validate a (well-formed) XML file against a nonmatching relaxNG file. If you change <element name="person"> to

`<element name="author">` in the file `quotes.rng`, the validation succeeds.

TIP: Creating a relaxNG file can be quite difficult; the Java tool Trang, available at http://thaiopensource.com/relaxng/trang.html, can read in an XML file and create a relaxNG, Schema, or DTD file out of it.

Validating a Schema is similar and is shown in the file `validate-xsd.php` in the download repository. When it comes to validating DTDs, you have to patch the XML a bit. The DTD file must be included in the file or referenced like this:

```
<!DOCTYPE note SYSTEM "quotes.dtd">
```

Then, just load the XML document into a DOM object and call `validate()`. The following contains the appropriate code; the file referenced in the code repository contains an intentional error in the DTD (`month` rather than `year`):

```php
<?php
  $dom = new DOMDocument();
  $dom->load('quotes-dtd.xml');
  echo 'Validation ' .
    (($dom->validate()) ? 'succeeded.' : 'failed.');
?>
```

Validating XML against a DTD (validate-dtd.php)

What Does PEAR Offer?

As of this writing, the XML section of the PHP Extension and Application Repository (PEAR) contains 35 packages, too many to mention. Here are some of them:

- `XML_Beautifier` formats XML documents so that they are prettier.
- `XML_DTD` allows parsing of DTDs, even with PHP 4.
- `XML_Parser2` provides an advanced XML parser.
- `XML_Serializer` converts XML files into data structures and vice versa.
- `XML_Util` contains a wealth of helper functions for working with XML.

11

Communicating with Others

Most of the previously discussed phrases worked within the ecosystem of the PHP script and the Web server in use. However, because some phrases can also be understood by others, this chapter covers some examples of this type. You can connect to remote servers in a variety of ways.

Connecting with HTTP Servers

```
<xmp>
<?php
  echo file_get_contents('http://www.php.net/');
?>
</xmp>
```

Reading in an HTTP Resource (http-file.php)

Hypertext Transfer Protocol (HTTP) is probably the protocol most often used from PHP to connect with others (apart from various database protocols). Starting with PHP 4.3, it is really easy to connect to such data sources because PHP's stream support was vastly improved in that version. (Of course, using HTTP in the way this code shows was already possible in earlier PHP releases.) The idea is that when you use a file operation, you access a stream of data. In practice, it doesn't really matter whether it's a file on the local system, on a network share, or on a remote server connected via either HTTP, File Transfer Protocol (FTP), or any other supported protocol. Just provide the appropriate filename, and PHP takes care of the rest. The preceding code shows this: It opens the PHP home page, and prints its Hypertext Markup Language (HTML) code in the browser. With just one line of code, it cannot get much more simple. Figure 11.1 contains the output.

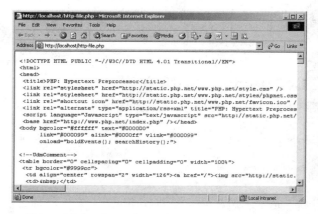

Figure 11.1   A one-liner prints the HTML markup of the PHP home page.

WARNING: For security reasons, you can turn off this behavior in php.ini by setting allow_url_fopen to Off; so, you cannot rely on it on Web servers you cannot control—for instance, shared hosting at large Internet service providers (ISPs).

If you want to control the HTTP request by yourself, you can do so by using sockets. First, use fsockopen() to open a socket to the Web server, and if that works, you then send a well-formed HTTP request. The following code implements this, again querying the PHP home page:

```php
<?php
  $fp = @fsockopen('www.php.net', 80, $errno,
➥$errstr, 30);
  if ($fp) {
    echo '<xmp>';
    $request = "GET / HTTP/1.0\r\n";
    $request .= "Host: www.php.net\r\n";
    $request .= "Connection: Close\r\n\r\n";
    fwrite($fp, $request);
    while (!feof($fp)) {
      echo fgets($fp, 1024);
    }
    fclose($fp);
    echo '</xmp>';
  } else {
    echo "Error: $errstr (#$errno)";
  }
?>
```

Reading in an HTTP Resource Using Sockets (http-socket.php)

The output is the same, with one difference: The socket approach also returns all HTTP headers sent by the server, whereas the stream wrappers omit them.

NOTE: When you must work with HTTP Secure (HTTPS) resources (Web sites secured with SSL [Secure Sockets Layer], for example), the two approaches still work, although with slight modification:

- When using file functions such as file_get_contents(), just provide an https:// uniform resource locator (URL).
- When using sockets, use an ssl:// URL.

Connecting with FTP Servers

```
file_get_contents('ftp://mirror.netcologne.de/
➥apache.org/httpd/README.html')
```

```php
<?php
  $data = file_get_contents('ftp://mirror.
➥netcologne.de/apache.org/httpd/README.html');
  file_put_contents('Apache-README.html', $data);
  echo 'File written.';
?>
```

Reading in an FTP File (ftp-file.php; excerpt)

When you are accessing FTP servers, PHP's stream wrappers come in very handy, as well. You only have read access, but the access is binary safe nonetheless. This code shows how to download the current README file for Apache from an FTP server and save it to the local hard disk using file_get_contents(). Writing is also possible; just use

`file_put_contents()` or the correct file mode for
`fopen()`. Note, though, that both reading and writing
simultaneously is not yet supported.

TIP: If you do not provide any credentials, PHP tries to
log you in to the FTP server using a guest account most
public FTP servers offer. You can, however, also provide
the credentials yourself:

```
$data = file_get_contents('ftp://USER:
➡PASSWORD@ftp.example.com/');
```

This works for HTTP resources (see previous phrase),
too!

PHP also comes with built-in support for FTP and a
special set of functions that implement the complete
FTP functionality defined in the associated Request For
Comment (RFC). In the Windows distributions, this is
enabled by default, whereas on other systems, PHP has
to be configured with the switch `--enable-ftp`. Then,
using the FTP server usually consists of the following
steps:

1. Connect to the server using `ftp_connect()`.

2. Log in using `ftp_login()`.

3. Go to the target directory using `ftp_chdir()`.

4. Read a file (`ftp_get()`) from or write a file
   (`ftp_put()`) to the FTP server.

5. Close the connection using `ftp_close()`.

Because reading is more common than writing, the following shows the former task being executed. Again,
the Apache README is fetched from an FTP server:

```php
<?php
  $ftp = @ftp_connect('mirror.netcologne.de');
  $login = @ftp_login($ftp, 'anonymous',
➥'email@example.com');

  if ($ftp && $login) {
    ftp_chdir($ftp, '/apache.org/httpd/ ');
    ftp_get($ftp, 'Apache-README-ftp.html',
➥'README.html', FTP_ASCII);
    echo 'File written.';
    ftp_close($ftp);
  } else {
    echo 'Error!';
  }
?>
```

*Reading in an FTP file Using the Built-In Functions
(ftp-functions.php)*

Note that the syntax of `ftp_get()` is a bit strange. After
the FTP resource, you first have to provide the local
filename, and then you must provide the remote filename. (Intuitively, you would expect it to be the other
way around.) The last parameter is the transfer mode:
`FTP_ASCII` for text files, and `FTP_BINARY` for all other
data.

Checking Whether a Server Is Still Reacting

```php
<?php
  $server = 'localhost';
  $port = '80';
  $status = 'unavailable';
```

```php
$fp = @fsockopen($server, $port, $errno, $errstr,
➥10);
if ($fp) {
  $status = 'alive, but not responding';
  fwrite($fp, "HEAD / HTTP/1.0\r\n");
  fwrite($fp, "Host: $server:$port\r\n\r\n");
  if (strlen(@fread($fp, 1024)) > 0) {
    $status = 'alive and kicking';
  }
  fclose($fp);
}
echo "The server is $status.";
?>
```

Checking the Status of a Server (serverstatus.php)

Suppose you have a Web server and you want to check periodically that it hasn't crashed again. In this scenario, using a PHP script for this task is a good idea. Just open a socket to the server and wait. (The last parameter of fsockopen() is a timeout value.) After this time has elapsed, you know whether the server is online or offline.

TIP: This works well if only one server's status must be checked. If there are several servers, this approach has some disadvantages. The call to fsockopen() might take up to the timeout value until the next command is executed. Therefore, all servers are checked sequentially and synchronously. This just takes too long for several servers. However, with PHP 5 and stream sockets, this can be done asynchronously. The code is a bit complicated, but Wez Furlong explains this approach in great detail at http://wezfurlong.org/blog/2005/may/guru-multiplexing/.

Understanding Web Services

Some people say Web Services are just old wine in new bottles because the idea behind them is far from new. The basic principle is this: Two machines talk to each other. For instance, one machine contains some business logic or, more generally, some information, and the other machine requests this information (or wants to use the business logic).

This has been done for many years, but only a few years ago the major players sat together and started to work on protocols to put the whole communication on top of standards. Some of these standards are now under the aegis of the World Wide Web Consortium (W3C), and others are managed by the Organization for the Advancement of Structured Information Standards (OASIS) consortium.

A number of books (many that are quite long) are available on Web Services. However, in accordance with the Phrasebook series methodology, this chapter keeps it short and simple, while still giving you all you need to know. A protocol is used to transfer both the request to the Web Service and its response. Several possibilities exist, but these two are most common:

- XML-RPC stands for Remote Procedure Call and uses a very simple XML dialect to transport function calls, parameters, and return values. This approach is sometimes tied to another concept called REST, for Representational State. There are some fierce debates about which approach is better, this protocol or the next one. Put simply, both have advantages (and disadvantages).

- SOAP once stood for Simple Object Access Protocol, but because it is neither simple nor has much to do with object access, today SOAP just stands for... SOAP. It is a rather complex protocol but overcomes many of the limitations of XML-RPC (which was, by the way, created by some parties who also worked on SOAP).

Most of the time, XML-RPC or SOAP calls are transported via HTTP as the carrier protocol. However, other protocols are also possible, including Simple Mail Transfer Protocol (SMTP) or even User Datagram Protocol (UDP).

When using SOAP, you need to consider one more important aspect: When you know exactly how a Web Service is implemented, you also know how to call (access or consume) it. However, many times this information is not available, so there must be a kind of self-description of the Web Service that contains all relevant information, such as which methods or functions are exposed, which parameters and data types they expect, and what they return. This can be done using a specifically crafted XML file, as well. The standard behind that is Web Services Description Language (WSDL). Today, WSDL is used for all relevant Web Services because it makes using them is quite simple. Most server-side technologies offer one way (or more) to just read in the WSDL and then access the Web Service as you would access a locally available class.

Generating all this XML is quite complicated. Not that PHP doesn't have good XML support, but the syntax can be quite hard. However, some extensions and external packages make using Web Services much easier. The following phrases each implement a Web Service that just adds two numbers. You will certainly be more imaginative and create some real-world Web Services based on what you learn in this chapter. In addition, we focus on SOAP web services; XML-RPC does not seem to be used that often these days, whereas JSON Web Services (which is covered later in this chapter) has become more popular.

Creating a Web Service with NuSOAP

```php
<?php
  require_once 'nusoap.php';

  $soap = new soap_server;
  $soap->register('add');
  $soap->service($HTTP_RAW_POST_DATA);

  function add($a, $b) {
    return $a + $b;
  }
?>
```

A SOAP Web Service with NuSOAP (soap-nusoap-server.php)

At http://nusoap.sourceforge.net/, you will find NuSOAP, one of the best-known external SOAP classes for PHP. Some might even know its predecessor, SOAPx4. These days, releases are not issued very often, but the library is quite stable. You might also want to check the Subversion (SVN) repository for the most recent code. You might find several files there, but nusoap.php is the one you want.

Creating a Web Service with NuSOAP is really simple because the module takes care of all the painful things, including SOAP. Just follow these steps:

1. Write the function you want to expose as a Web method.

2. Instantiate the `soap_server` class.

3. Register your function with the SOAP server.

4. Call the `service()` method and submit `$HTTP_RAW_POST_DATA` as the parameter.

This code implements a SOAP server using NuSOAP. Figure 11.2 shows the output in the browser when you are trying to call the Web Service directly from the client. The error message says that the XML was empty—of course it is, because we didn't send a request!

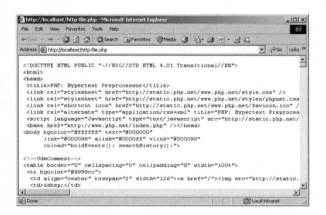

Figure 11.2   This error message is a good sign; the script seems to work (so far).

Automatically Generating WSDL with NuSOAP

```php
<?php
  require_once 'nusoap.php';

  $soap = new soap_server;
  $soap->configureWSDL('AddService',
➥'http://php.phrasebook.org/');
  $soap->wsdl->schemaTargetNamespace =
➥'http://soapinterop.org/xsd/';
  $soap->register(
    'add',
    array('a' => 'xsd:int', 'b' => 'xsd:int'),
    array('c' => 'xsd:int'),
    'http://soapinterop.org/'
  );
  $soap->service(isset($HTTP_RAW_POST_DATA) ?
➥$HTTP_RAW_POST_DATA : '');

  function add($a, $b) {
    return $a + $b;
  }
?>
```

A WSDL-Enabled Web Service with NuSOAP
(wsdl-nusoap-server.php)

As mentioned previously, current Web Services almost always use WSDL. Writing WSDL manually is a real pain and very error prone, but most serious Web Services implementations for PHP can create WSDL automatically. However, because PHP is not a strongly typed language, the Web Services need some help.

To do so with NuSOAP, the code from the previous section must be expanded a bit. First, a method `configureWSDL()` must be called to provide the name and the namespace of the service. Then, the signature of the method must be provided (which parameters go in, which go out). Then, the server is started. However, this time whether `$HTTP_RAW_POST_DATA` is set is checked or not. This is because when it is not set, the user has made a GET request, so the user might just want the WSDL description.

Back to the WSDL: Figure 11.3 shows the Web Service in the browser when called using GET. A click on the link shows some information about the `add()` method. In Figure 11.4, you see what happens when you append `?WSDL` to the URL of the script (or click on the WSDL link): The WSDL for the service is automatically generated. Imagine if you had to do this manually!

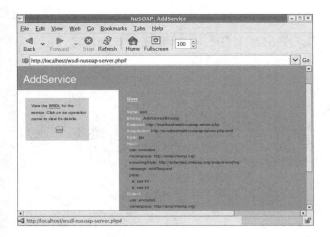

Figure 11.3 Now NuSOAP automatically generates an info page for the service.

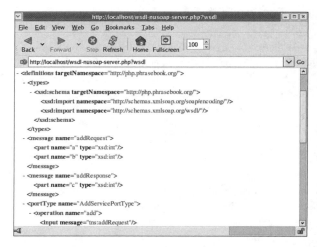

Figure 11.4 This WSDL is generated by NuSOAP, not by the programmer.

Consuming a Web Service with NuSOAP

```php
<?php
  require_once 'nusoap.php';

  $soap = new soapclient('http://localhost/
➥wsdl-nusoap-server.php?wsdl', true);
  $proxy = $soap->getProxy();
  $result = $proxy->add(47, 11);
  echo "47 + 11 = $result";
?>
```

*Consuming the Web Service with NuSOAP
(wsdl-nusoap-client.php)*

Actually, using a NuSOAP service is even easier than creating one. You just have to load the WSDL file and then get a so-called proxy class. (That's a local class that behaves just as if the Web Service is a local class, too.) So, you can call the Web Service's methods directly, and NuSOAP takes care of all the rest (including opening a connection to the remote server, assembling and parsing XML, and so on).

To do this, the `soapclient` class (without the underscore character) must be instantiated, and then the `getProxy()` method creates the proxy class. The code implements this for the demo service from the previous example. Note the URL of the WSDL file: It's the Web Service's URL plus `?wsdl` appended to the end; change the URL accordingly for your system.

NOTE: Appending ?wsdl to the URL to get the WSDL description of a Web Service is an idea borrowed from Microsoft .NET (and now also used in other technologies). However, there the appendix is not case sensitive, whereas NuSOAP requires it to be in lowercase letters. Keep this in mind when working cross-platform.

Creating a Web Service with the PHP 5 SOAP Extension

```php
<?php
  $soap = new SoapServer(null, array('uri' =>
➥'http://php.phrasebook.org/'));
  $soap->addFunction('add');
  $soap->handle();
```

```
  function add($a, $b) {
    return $a + $b;
  }
?>
```

A Web Service with PHP 5 SOAP (soap-php5-server.php)

One of the key features of PHP 5 is the new SOAP extension. Because it is written in C, it is much faster than anything that is coded in PHP alone. However, the extension is relatively new, so there are still some hiccups and missing features. However, it often works well.

You have to configure PHP with --enable-soap to use the extension; Windows users have to add extension=php_soap.dll to their php.ini configuration file. Then, the extension is available, and writing a SOAP server is quite easy.

Again, it's a small number of steps: Instantiate the SoapServer class, add your function with addFunction(), and, finally, call handle().

Automatically Generating WSDL with the PHP 5 SOAP Extension

The greatest shortcoming of PHP 5 SOAP is that there is no way to automatically generate WSDL with it. This is not often mentioned; however, it does create problems in real life. WSDL is so complicated that errors in the WSDL are hard to see and even harder to find.

However, you can create such a WSDL description for a Web Service in several ways, most of which have been used in real-world projects:

- Use NuSOAP or PEAR::SOAP to create a similar service, just to get the WSDL—just change the `<soap:address>` element
- Use the class `Ctrx_SOAP_AutoDiscover` (available at http://crtx.org/index.php?area=Main&page=Crtx SoapAutoDiscover)
- Use the Webservice Helper tool (available at http://www.jool.nl/new/index.php?file_id=1)
- Use the `WSDL_Gen` class (available at http://www.schlossnagle.org/~george/php/ WSDL_Gen.tgz)

So you can see, WSDL support is being worked on, not as part of the SOAP extension itself, but in the form of external projects. Hopes are that this will change some day.

If you finally have a WSDL description of your service (in the download archive, you will find a file `AddService.wsdl` that originated from the PEAR::SOAP-generated WSDL), the code for the server has to be updated just slightly. The first parameter for the `SoapServer` instantiation receives the WSDL URL; in addition, the methods of the Web Service must be put in a class. Then, `setClass()` provides the SOAP extension with the name of the class to be used:

```php
<?php
  $soap = new SoapServer(
    'AddService.wsdl',
    array('uri' => 'http://php.phrasebook.org/')
  );
  $soap->setClass('ServiceClass');
  $soap->handle();

  class ServiceClass {
```

```
    function add($a, $b) {
      return $a + $b;
    }
  }
?>
```

A WSDL-Enabled Web Service with NuSOAP
(wsdl-php5-server.php)

Consuming a Web Service with the PHP 5 SOAP Extension

```
<?php
  $soap = new SoapClient('AddService.wsdl');
  try {
    $result = $soap->add(47, 11);
    echo "47 + 11 = $result";
  } catch (SoapFault $e) {
    echo "Error: {$e->faultstring}";
  }
}
```

Consuming the Web Service with PHP 5 SOAP
(wsdl-php5-client.php)

Consumption is again easy, as long as you have a WSDL description. This code calls the Web Services and also catches any errors, thanks to PHP 5's try-catch mechanism.

TIP: In an attempt to boost performance, PHP 5's SOAP extension defaults to caching WSDL. The following are the standard settings from php.ini-recommended:

```
[soap]
; Enables or disables WSDL caching feature.
soap.wsdl_cache_enabled=1
; Sets the directory name where SOAP extension
➥will put cache files.
soap.wsdl_cache_dir="/tmp"
; (time to live) Sets the number of seconds while
➥cached file will be used
; instead of original one.
soap.wsdl_cache_ttl=86400
```

When developing a Web Service and maybe changing the WSDL, this is, of course, a no-brainer. Therefore, set soap.wsdl_cache_enabled to Off during development, but turn it on for production servers.

Using Ajax

Wikipedia lists several dozen different meanings for the term *Ajax*, including a soccer team from the Netherlands, two figures in Homer's *Iliad*, and a household-cleaning product. However, since 2005, Ajax also stands for Asynchronous JavaScript + XML. The technology is far from new (the underlying technology, XML HTTP requests from JavaScript, is supported by recent versions of Internet Explorer, Firefox, Safari, and Chrome—also, XML is not required at all for this), but only after this weird term was coined did people actually start using it.

The basic principle is that JavaScript can now call a remote server and then process its return values without having to reload the whole page. Of course, this has little to do with PHP; however, some Ajax classes make using Ajax from within PHP very easy.

This phrase shows a very short demonstration of Ajax. This phrase uses the Sajax toolkit (the *S* stands for *simple*) available at www.modernmethod.com/sajax/. Many Ajax libraries and frameworks are available, so feel free to pick the one you like most; we are just picking a simple one here to focus on the combination of Ajax and PHP.

The complete code for this example is quite long because both PHP and JavaScript are needed. First, you need the server-side logic. For this, the Sajax toolkit is loaded, which comes as a single PHP file. You then "export" (register) all PHP functions you want to use from the client side. The following example has a small function that generates a random RGB color:

```php
<?php
  require_once 'Sajax.php';

  sajax_init();
  sajax_export('randomColor');
  sajax_handle_client_request();

  function randomColor() {
    $color = '#';
    for ($i=0; $i<3; $i++) {
      $color .= dechex(rand(0, 255));
    }
    return $color;
  }
?>
```

The Server-Side Part of the Application (ajax.php; excerpt)

On the client side, a call to the (PHP) function `sajax_show_javascript()` does most of the work; it creates some lines of JavaScript code that take care of the requests to the Web server in the background. Then, all PHP functions that have been registered before can be called on the client side by prepending x_ to the name of the function. One parameter you have to provide is the name of a callback function; this function is then called when the server side has responded to the request.

The following code calls the randomColor() PHP function every five seconds and then writes a text in this random color—all without server round-trips! Figure 11.5 shows the result:

```
<script type="text/javascript">
<?php
  sajax_show_javascript();
?>
  changeColor();
  setInterval(changeColor, 5000);

  function changeColor() {
    x_randomColor(randomColor_callback);
  }

  function randomColor_callback(result) {
    var text = '<span style="color: ' + result +
➡';">A colorful acronym ...</span>';
    document.getElementById('output').innerHTML =
➡text;
  }
</script>
...
<div id="output"></div>
```

The Client-Side Part of the Application (ajax.php; excerpt)

Figure 11.5   The text appears, thanks to
JavaScript code calling PHP.

Exchanging Data with the Server

In the preceding phrase, the data we exchanged with
the server was quite trivial—a simple string. In real-
world applications, however, we have more complex
data we need to send from the client to the server and
back. XML could be used as an exchange format,
but it is bloated, and so does not fare well with high-
performance applications. PHP's serialize() and
unserialize() methods could be used to convert complex information into a string that can be exchanged
via HTTP, but there is no built-in counterpart functionality JavaScript offers.

The de facto standard for data exchange with
JavaScript is JSON, JavaScript Object Notation. The
unofficial home page at http://json.org/ explains the
format in great detail, but basically JSON sums up the

part of the JavaScript specification where arrays are
explained. Take this string, for instance:

```
[
  {"url": "http:\/\/json.org\/", "text": "JSON"},
  {"url": "http:\/\/php.net\/", "text": "PHP"}
]
```

This is the syntax that can be used within JavaScript to
define an array that contains two associative arrays (or
objects, as some call it, despite these elements not really
being objects). Modern browsers have an easy built-in
functionality to convert such a string into a real
JavaScript value (and there are workarounds for older
versions), so JSON is ideal for Ajax applications.

Beginning with version 5.2, PHP supports JSON out
of the box. The function `json_encode()` converts a seri-
alizable PHP value into JSON, and `json_decode()` converts a JSON string back into something PHP can
work with. The following code essentially creates the
preceding JSON string, minus the indentations and
extra whitespace characters:

```php
<?php

  class LinkData {
    public $url;
    public $text;
    public function __construct($url, $text) {
      $this->url = $url;
      $this->text = $text;
    }
  }

  $data = array(
    new LinkData('http://json.org/', 'JSON'),
```

```
    new LinkData('http://php.net/', 'PHP')
  );

  echo json_encode($data);

?>
```

The JSON Server Endpoint (json.php)

On the client side, JavaScript code can then call the PHP
script and process the data. When using a JavaScript library
like the popular jQuery (http://jquery.com/), working
with the JSON data can be quite easy (see Figure 11.6).
The following code displays the information contained in
the JSON string in the form of a bulleted list:

```
<script type=""text/javascript"
➥src="http://code.jquery.com/jquery-
➥latest.js"></script>
<script type=""text/javascript">
$(function() {
  $.getJSON("json.php", function(data) {
    $.each(data, function(key, value) {
      $("<a>").attr("href", value.url)
              .html(value.text)
              .wrap("<li>")
              .parent()
              .appendTo("ul");
    });
  });
});
</script>
...
<body>
  <ul></ul>
</body>
```

The JSON Client, Using jQuery (json.html)

Figure 11.6   The JSON data is parsed and
then displayed as a list, thanks to jQuery calling
PHP code.

What Does PEAR Offer?

Along with the several modules mentioned in this
chapter, the following PHP Extension and Application
Repository (PEAR) packages offer functionality that can
be helpful when connecting with others using PHP:

- The HTTP category of PEAR offers some
  relevant packages, including HTTP, HTTP_Header,
  HTTP_Request2, and HTTP_Server.
- Likewise, you can find useful packages in the
  Networking category, including Net_FTP, Net_IMAP,
  and Net_Socket.
- The Services category of PEAR contains several
  classes that offer an easy-to-use interface for
  well-known Web Services.

Index

0083   11